Santayana, George
The idler and his
works

THE IDLER AND HIS WORKS

and other essays

THE IDLER
AND HIS WORKS

AND OTHER ESSAYS

by George Santayana

EDITED AND WITH A PREFACE BY

Daniel Cory

1957

George Braziller, Inc.

NEW YORK

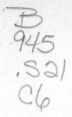

PREFACE

THE ESSAYS GATHERED in this volume have never appeared in book form, and several of them not even in periodicals. They represent various aspects of Santayana's many-colored mind, and reveal those ruling civilized interests that found expression in more than sixty years of unique and beautiful writing.

In the first part I have placed two mature essays of capital importance. "The Idler and His Works" was composed during the last war, when Santayana was shut off in Rome from all contact with the free world. It is a masterpiece of its kind in which he attempts to sum up his life's literary labors and evaluate them from the standpoint of posterity. It is as if he said: "This is how I see myself and my work *sub specie aeternitatis*."

The essay on "Americanism" was written sometime between 1935 and 1940. Santayana did not publish it at once, because he felt that perhaps some of his admonitions and strictures on our way of thinking and living were a little harsh, and he wanted time to reconsider the whole matter. Then in the summer of 1952 in Rome (a few months before he died) he handed me this essay and asked me to take good care of it. He said it was "up to me" to do whatever I thought best. He added, however, "I don't

v

think it will hurt the American people to be scolded a bit: they are too cheeky!"

The second part comprises a group of reviews and interpretations of other distinguished thinkers. With the exception of the essay on Spengler, they were composed around the turn of the century when Santayana was one of the leading lights at Harvard. They are interesting for two reasons. Firstly, they are of value for their criticism and appreciation of classic philosophers like Plato and Spinoza, or more recent figures like William James, Croce and Spengler. And secondly, for lovers of Santayana, they are fascinating as examples of his early literary style and development of life-long interests.

The third part is essential for students of Santayana's deliberate *system of philosophy*. The long essay "On Metaphysical Projection," for example, is a profound piece of historical analysis—whether or not we agree with its main distinctions or accept without reservation the interpretations of Indian philosophy, German Transcendentalism, and the theory of relativity. This essay is really a kind of supplementary Introduction to *Realms of Being*, inasmuch as it contains Santayana's mature system of philosophy in a nutshell. The essay on "The Coming Philosophy," will repay study as a devastating criticism of the philosophical movement in America known as the New or Neo-Realism.

And last but not least, there is a lovely little dialogue "On Immortality," to close this volume of diverse but representative essays on an appropriate theme.

DANIEL CORY

Bexhill on Sea, Sussex 1956

ACKNOWLEDGMENTS

THE ESSAYS LISTED below originally appeared in the following periodicals, and acknowledgment is herewith made for permission (where necessary) to include them in this book.

"The Idler and His Works," *Saturday Review*, May 15, 1954
"Americanism," *Virginia Quarterly Review*, Winter issue, 1955
"Search for the True Plato," *The International Monthly*, Feb., 1902
"Ethical Doctrine of Spinoza," *Harvard Monthly*, June, 1886
"Spengler," *The New Adelphi*, March, 1929
"James's Psychology," *Atlantic Monthly*, 1892
"Croce's Aesthetics," *Journal of Comparative Literature*, April, 1903
"The Coming Philosophy," *Journal of Philosophy*, August 13, 1914
"On Immortality," *Virginia Quarterly Review*, Winter issue, 1954

CONTENTS

CONTENTS

THE IDLER AND HIS WORKS

and other essays

THE IDLER
AND HIS WORKS

MANY OTHER PERSONS and places not mentioned in this book have played important parts in my life and left their ghosts, at night, in my dreams: but they had better remain there. I have recorded here only such fragments of biography as still interested my waking mind, or perhaps might serve some antiquary curious about the times or the types that I have painted with care. Many of them, although potent influences over me in my private capacity, may seem insignificant and tiresome to a reader who thinks of me as an author: and how else should a reader think of me? Yet it is not at all as an author or as a professional philosopher that I think of myself. I have written a great many books and a great many reviews and articles. Astonishing bibliographies of them have been compiled, astonishing, I mean to me; I wonder how I found time for wasting so much ink and paper. I have seldom been conscious of working hard. Most of my writing has been an instinctive pleasure, a playful impulse, as in running down a grassy slope or exploring a wood-

3

land path. The things wrote themselves; and when I dropped the pen, and rose from my writing-table, I seemed to awake from a trance and to be myself again. Yet that other dreaming, industrious self, weaving words eagerly together, and excogitating arguments and opinions as if he were an animated book, is doubtless the self that I am supposed to be and that, in an autobiography, I should have been expected to write about.

No doubt that industrious, playful, automatic self was an original part of me, and a persistent part. I am happy in mental idleness, with manual work. I envy the house-maids, so common in Southern Europe, who sing as they scrub. I feel that there is something sane and comfortable in the old women, who sit knitting, or turning over the roasting chestnuts at the street corners. I like to spend drowsy hours drawing, cleaning or making something, or even mending my clothes. Pleasant is solitude among man-ageable things. And among manageable things, the most manageable for me are words. All my life, since I re-gained my freedom, I have passed the morning writing. The theme had been chosen in a moment of inspiration. The chapter, perhaps the paragraph, was already begun. Nothing was required but to turn on the current, if only the current would come, and continue the flow of lan-guage. The material act of writing entertained me; also the semi-material act of arranging and re-arranging the words. Often the thought was rekindled in the process, transformed, sharpened, corrected; and out came an epi-gram or a terse formula for something that had perhaps been floating in my mind for years.

Various peculiarities and faults of my writings are due to this mechanical and dreamful way of composing them. All is improvised, as in poetry: hence, unless there is a drastic revision, so much repetition, so much that is desultory, rambling, inconclusive. No strict program, no order was predetermined, no precise limits or scope. Such a method or lack of method would have been fatal had there not been sharp definition in my thought, clear principles in my judgments. As it is, though the surface be sometimes confused, as in a tapestry, the figures at a little distance stand out clearly enough; and I think that, at least in my later works, a sympathetic reader will not be seriously troubled by my meanderings. The mountains and the sea are never out of sight. I don't stop to reconsider what comes to me as I write, and I consult no authorities; but I have read much and reflected long before I begin writing.

As regards the subject-matter my work might be divided into two strands, the poetic and the academic. There may be poetic touches and irresponsible flights sometimes in the academic books, and academic themes even in the poetry: yet the two were originally quite distinct. My verses and my private philosophizing belonged to me, expressed me, and were addressed essentially to nobody else; the academic subjects were suggested or imposed by circumstances, and I appear there in the costume and under the mask of an assumed character. The acting is sincere enough, but the part is conventional. My life does not appear in my works until we turn to *Poems, Soliloquies in England, Dialogues in Limbo* and *The Last Puritan*. In these my inmost feelings, and the places and persons concerned in my real life, supply the subject and control the expression. It is not a question of complete portraits (hardly ever in this book) either of myself or of others. All has been recast in a crucible, and there appear only possibilities, dream-images of my surroundings and passions, such as the mind retains more willingly than the accidental and imperfect realities.

In the academic books, besides the rhetorical veneer that I have spoken of, there is a tendency to infuse more and more of myself into the apprehension of the world and of its opinions, until in *Realms of Being* the picture of them becomes itself a confession and an image of the mind that composed it. Not that I have intentionally indulged the imagination here, as in the poems and the novel: on the contrary, I have studied to be austere and sceptical and to discount the human mind and its bias as far as possible. But this love of the bare truth, this intellectual asceticism, is itself a human passion and the secret of a regenerate life: so that the more I strip myself of myself, the better I bring to light that something in me that is more myself than I am—the spirit. I believe there is substantial though relative truth in my philosophy, since it is merely the confession of sincere and fundamental assumptions, which a living being can hardly avoid; and I hope that some more powerful and better-knit mind may arise and restate those views as I ought to have stated them. But that could be done in a single volume, without any of the accidental trappings that encumber my compositions. All my technical writings could then be forgotten to advantage, even as my own mind prefers to forget them.

When by chance I open one of my books, especially one of the earlier ones, it seems to me the work of some other man; and I am surprised if I come to something that sounds like what I should say myself. In general the tone and tenor remain quite foreign to me. Not that I have changed my opinions. I should still say the same things, did the same questions present themselves to me in the same terms. But those terms belonged to a fundamentally foreign morality. I said in them, as well as I could, what I honestly felt; yet they constituted a literary and diplomatic veil to my latent intelligence. I seemed cold (as Bertrand Russell has observed) when my heart was burning away beneath the embers; and it has taken the greater part of a long life for me to extricate my meaning from my words, find the center of my survey, and form fresh categories and a fresh vocabulary.

Ancient philosophy was a great aid to me in this: the more I retreated in time, and the farther east I looked, the more I discovered my own profound and primitive convictions. The conventional moralizing and the prim aesthetic judgments of my earlier books need not be contradicted; the literary psychology in them may even be confirmed; but all this needs to be grounded in physical facts and at the same time shown to be purely relative to special phases of human life and to special predicaments. The surface of human experience must not be taken for its ground or for its own motive power. It is all an effect of sub-human or super-human forces. The liberal, empirical, psychological philosophy into which I was plunged was miserably artificial, like a modern town laid out in squares. There was nothing subterranean acknowledged in it, no ultimate catastrophe, no jungle, no desert, and no laughter of the Gods. Mankind lived lost in the fog of self-consciousness, persuaded that it was creating itself and the whole universe. They had forgotten their religion; and their philosophy, when they had one, was a glorification of their vanity and of their furious impulse to make money, to make machines, and to make war. What would come of it, except perhaps to make them all alike? In my solitude I watched their mechanical arts not without admiration: they were clever children making their own toys, and as busy at it as birds building their nests or worms burrowing their holes. Verily they have their reward, if they enjoy the process. But may they not be rather multiplying their troubles, and missing the natural pleasures and dignity of man? These pleasures and dignity lie in seeing and thinking, in living with an understanding of the place and destiny of life.

Now reflection convinces me that what is called experience, the obvious and inescapable pressure of sensation, is intrinsically a dream, something arbitrary, fugitive, unsubstantial, coming out of nothing and ending in nothing. Yet since this dream is endured, and to some extent may be surveyed and remembered, there is something else on the hither side of it which I call the spirit; a witness, but not an agent, since spirit can neither bring the dream about nor avoid it nor understand why it should come.

8

This coming, however, is a terrible assault to the spirit, for it awakes in terror and tears; so that, on the further side of the dream and antecedent to it, there is something dynamic, obscure to the spirit, but overwhelmingly powerful and real, which I call matter, but which, if you prefer, you may call God. Spirit here and matter or God there are not phenomena; they are not distinguishable and recognizable features in the dream, but an outlying power in the one case and an observant intellect in the other, which is not observed but is analytically implied in the fact of observation and in the act of comparing one part of the dream with another and noting its inconstancy and confusion.

The terms employed in this apprehension of experience remain mere images or words, but for intelligence they become signs for something beneath or beyond them, matter, God or spirit, of which they manifest the presence, power and method of action. Such manifestation, however, is not exhaustive, as if the words or images were alone real, and signified nothing further. They do not define their object but only indicate it. Nothing existent can be defined. Definition defines only the idea, the word, or the image: the object is transcendent. Matter, God or spirit have to be posited beyond. Only such substances, powers or faculties can have any depth or persistence or can render our visions and definitions valid or true of anything beyond themselves.

Such was the summary system of categories by which in the end I cleared my mind, at least in principle and in intention, of all foreign confusion. In fact, however, the books in which I worked out that system—*Scepticism and Animal Faith* and *Realms of Being*—are terribly overloaded with accidental matters, the mud and the weeds that clung to me as I struggled out of the bog. Nevertheless, I hope that a benevolent reader will shed these impedimenta as he advances, and will retain at the end a clear sense of my *radical position*. It is not at all new or artificial. I did not reach it by invention or hypothesis but by retreat from all inventions and hypotheses to the inevitable assumptions and the obvious terms of all apprehension. Then I found myself reverting to a system like those of the first Greek philosophers, who looked at the world boldly, without religious preconceptions, yet found it to be much the same world that the Indians described in their religious meditations. But the Indian like the Christian philosophers were encumbered with fantastic notions, suggested by moral predicaments to an unrestrained imagination; and it is necessary to remove these problems to the moral and poetical sphere where they belong. They are human problems and a man may well find them more interesting and important than cosmology, but this poetic or moral enthusiasm in him will not change the real conditions of his life, or the source and development of that enthusiasm itself; so that, even in the interests of his private spiritual progress, he will do well in the first place not to deceive himself about his natural status. Nothing could be farther from me than a desire to quench the imagination; on the contrary I would preserve it in all its freedom and originality. But it should not profess to be perception or science, if it would not become madness.

My philosophical system, being thus discovered within me, was latent in all the earlier phases of my opinions; and I think there is very little in my first writings that cannot be inserted into my mature system. Yet I was not clearly aware, when I wrote those innocent phrases, in what sense exactly they ought to be understood; so that some uncertainty and confusion seems to hang about my words. The words came from the heart, I was always sincere; but the heart was reacting upon alien impressions, and not speaking freely out of its clear depths. It would be necessary in each case to understand the circumstances and the connections in which such thoughts came into my mind; and then the spontaneous side of my reaction, which alone would express my innate philosophy, could be disengaged.

In my first prose book, *The Sense of Beauty*, the argument is uninspired and academic; I was writing the book for a practical purpose. Yet it was I that was writing it; so that in the incidental touches and in the style there is more of me than in the doctrine. I speak as if the sense of beauty were compounded of ingredients, so much sugar, so much lemon and so much water making the proper lemonade. But sensations are moments of spirit, they cannot endure, they cannot be compounded; and the whole "chemistry of mind" goes on in the psyche, in the life of the body, from which the richest and subtlest intuition issues pure and whole, like the sound of a bell, or the voice singing. I had not yet read Aristotle sufficiently or understood that the psyche is the life of the body as a whole, in its unity and direction, partially and incidentally expressed in consciousness. When I spoke of "objectified pleasure," apart from the false subsistence apparently attributed to feelings, as if they could be tossed about like dice in a dicebox, there was nevertheless a true sense of the nerve of perception, which is transcendent intent or indication: the psyche receives an impression, and the intellect and will respond with a belief. So in the presence of things harmonious with its life, the psyche luxuriates and is suffused with a vital pleasure; a part of this pleasure may be proper to the act of seeing or hearing, which at the same time evokes a visual or musical image: and since this image is a recognizable object our joy in it comes as the sense of its beauty, not as a sense of our pleasure. The beauty is probably the first thing felt by the lover, before the form in which it dwells becomes distinct and articulate in his vision. So the sun attracts and dazzles us, before we can focus the eyes on its color or its shape.

In turning to criticism, as I did in *Interpretations of Poetry and Religion*, I began to rescue the part that was my own from the borrowed part of my philosophy. The themes were public, and principally drawn from English literature and philosophy; but now the judgments passed, and the criterion that inspired them, were frankly not English. What were they? We cannot say that they were Spanish or Catholic, yet they lay in that direction; in that direction and beyond, in the humanism not of the Renaissance but of antiquity. The Renaissance was not a re-birth but a reproduction of relics; the seeds of antiquity had not been replanted in the soil of Christendom, so that they might bloom afresh into a new and complete life. There had been merely a revival, a restauration—patches of antiquity inserted in the torn garment of the Christian mind. Now in my criticism, I was falling back upon pre-Christian, merely human standards; yet these in one sense were even more Christian than the English standard of appreciation. They condemned "the poetry of barbarism," the worship of impulse, enterprise, effort and blind adventure. They were anti-romantic, anti-idealistic, and demanded a "life of reason."

The long book in which I expounded what I conceived a life of reason to be suffered from the very faults that my criticism condemned: it was too impulsive, too pretentious, too casual, and based on too little learning. Admiration of ancient Greece and modern England insinuated a didactic tone into the political part, and made me seem a prophet of I don't know what Utopia. This tone pleased people in America, especially the young Jews, and perhaps caused the book to become well known in that circle when otherwise it might have been altogether neglected. It also caused the book to be misinterpreted, as if it had been inspired by romantic idealism and not grounded, as it was meant to be, on a materialistic view of nature and life. Such a view does not exclude the possibility of all sorts of beautiful and surprising developments in the universe. The natural world is indefinitely fertile; but its fertility is not directed by the human will; it is not governed, except in man, by human interests. The sentiment that it would justly inspire about human life and human hopes would be extremely sober. Beings that arise are likely to find means of subsistence and a chance to propagate their kind, because otherwise they would never have arisen; but in no particular case, and at no particular time, can a race or an individual be sure of continued good fortune; and no specific hope about distant issues is ever likely to be realized. The ground shifts, the will of mankind deviates, and what the father dreamt of, the children neither fulfil nor desire.

My political fancy had undergone two love-affairs, two seasons in which I almost believed that I had discovered the ideal in the real. Greece and England had seemed to me, in different directions, to have come near it. I called it the life of reason. By this I meant that on the one hand the world had been conceived sanely in effect, though in poetical or rhetorical terms; on the other hand the art of life had been developed in two different directions, each of them satisfying. But satisfying to whom? In Greece to the Greeks and in England to the English? Or in both, ideally, to me? On this point I had not come to clearness. If I meant that the ideals suggested to me by Greece and England, somehow fused together, seemed to me to satisfy all the just demands of human nature, then my long book on *The Life of Reason* should have painted a concrete picture of a perfect society. I should have constructed another Utopia. But I possessed neither the varied knowledge nor the firm principles requisite for such a performance. My book was only a semi-historical, semi-judicial review of the most familiar forms of society, religion, art and science in the western world; and while a rational criterion of moral judgment did underlie the whole discussion, this criterion was not clearly set forth or strictly applied. My mind was allowed to float lazily amongst plausible opinions. I intended, however, to be a consistent naturalist, and I ought to have smiled a little at my casual enthusiasms, seeing that all ideals are but projections of vital tendencies in animal organisms. Therefore, since animal organisms are of many variable sorts, the direction and goal of progress always remain optional and subject to revision. This would have reduced my lovely Greece and my lovely England to local episodes in the history of manners and morals. Their rightness would have been avowedly only relative, even if it had been complete. But it had been sadly incomplete. Soon experience in the case of England and a little more reading in the case of Greece brought my two political love-affairs to an end.

This book, though loosely composed and imperfectly digested, still marks an advance from convention to radical sincerity. I perceived that morality is something normal, and that religion, like perception, clothes in spontaneous sensuous or imaginative signs the real presence of pressing dangers and favorable opportunities. The material world and our animal nature, far from being obstacles in our way, are indispensable conditions for the pursuit and safe possession of any good; indispensable indeed for the discrimination of good from evil, or their existence at all. There must be something not chosen that chooses, something not desired that desires. This dynamic surd, this primeval automatism, within us and without, sustains the whole ideal structure of our language, our thoughts, and our interests, keeps them consecutive and brings forth the fruits that we promise ourselves and the catastrophes that we wish to avoid.

Of historical illustrations for this thesis the best I had to offer were drawn from religion. There I had more information and more experience than in other spheres. I was at home in the workings of *la fonction fabulatrice*. Moreover, I knew the difference between well-grounded inspired myths, innocently mistaken for revelations, and the vapid fancies of stray poets. In both cases we suffer illusion, because passion, and often action, reacts upon an image as if it were a physical object. But the illusion proper to waking perception and to wise myths, when once discovered, drives us all the more confidently and successfully upon the real object; whereas the illusion proper to idle musings and dreams leaves us cheated and disaffected towards reality. A great religion need not fear philosophic criticism, which will liberate its moral and speculative substance from the poetic images in which it first appeared. Ultimate truths are more easily and adequately conveyed by poetry than by analysis. This is no reason for forbidding analysis, but it is a reason for not banishing poetry.

My later books teach the same lesson, but by a different approach. They may seem to move in the opposite direction; yet only because they start from an opposite quarter in making for the same goal. This goal is a good life, according to our nature and circumstances; and it may be missed either by ignoring it or misconceiving our true circumstances or else by ignoring or misconceiving our true nature and proper good. Now for a mind coming to philosophy from religion and poetry, as I did, and as did the first Greek philosophers, the pressing reform seems to be to criticize anthropomorphism in religion and fable in science; to insist that life, reason, and spirit are something natural, and that it is only by facing our true environment, and making the best of it, that we can develop them well. Therefore those early Greek philosophers, who were great poets and prophets of nature, figured as sour enemies of mythology: and so I too, whose turn of mind was always poetical and religious, seemed to discard all inspiration and idealism. Yet when naturalism in regard to circumstances had been firmly rooted in my mind, the other half of the total problem spontaneously came to the fore. What, in this natural world, is the nature and possible virtue of man? On what, without folly and intimate disaster, can he set his heart? And I was constrained to reply: Only on the life of reason, only on union with the truth, only on ideal sympathy with that irrepressible spirit which comes to light in all living beings, flowering differently in each, and moving in each towards a special perfection. And allowing for the different background introduced by my naturalism, this was very like the reply given by the most radical religious teachers, idealists, and mystics: so that I might seem to be moving away from my earlier doctrine and reverting to the traditions that I had rejected. Yet I was not in the least reverting to the illusions about circumstances that accompanied those traditions; I was merely placing the spirit, the motives and the discipline found in those traditions back where they belonged:

for they were all voices of nature, elicited by human predicaments.

How rich and how full of significance in regard to the natural world and to human life in it this spiritual music may be, I have attempted to show once more in what may well be my last book on *The Idea of Christ in the Gospels, or God in Man.* There is less presumption than we might at first suspect in taking Christ for a model after having identified him with God. Reason differs from perception and sentiment precisely in transcending our human egotism and aspiring to understand things as they are in themselves and to love in them the good that they love. This aspiration of reason extends inevitably to sharing the vision and judgments of God; in other words, to transporting ourselves into the presence of the truth and to living, as Aristotle says, as much as possible in the eternal. Omniscience can neither lose nor expect anything, and lives exclusively in the vision of all things under the form of eternity. A corollary of this teaches us that it is only ideally that things can enter the mind. When passing events enter the mind they stick there: they become ideas of those events. Now it is in memory and imagination that we know the world: while we move in it, if memory and inspiration do not retain any images of it, we are simply a part of the moving world and know nothing of it. Physical life perforce keeps time with the rest of the physical world and is in flux like it. But reason bridges those gaps and makes a panorama of those variations. Though it is impossible for us to live our lives all at once, we may cultivate a sense of its totality, and of the totality and truth of things. In that measure we shall have lived, as it were, in the presence of God, and in as full harmony with his vision and will as our human nature allows.

Let me repeat, however, that I do not propose this sublimation of the life of reason as something obligatory: no man can achieve it completely, and most men can hardly practice it at all. I see nothing wrong or sad in that. It is right that most of what we are and of what we think should be lost for ever. Eternal damnation overtakes it justly. Society will judge some minds to be too flighty and others to be too rigid or too mystical; but those judgments have only a relative authority. It may be true that such habits are inconvenient for certain purposes: but no man's and no society's convenience can remake or limit the world. It is always lawful for a butterfly to be a butterfly, and it is lawful for a man like La Fontaine to be proud of being a butterfly, as when he says:

Je suis chose légère et vole à tout sujet:
Je vais de fleur en fleur et d'objet en objet.

Yet the butterflies had better not form a league to exterminate the sages. The sages will smile upon them, and survive.

In spite of being so much in sympathy with the sages, I am well aware of not having been one of them. As a person I was too self-indulgent and not heroic enough; as a writer I was too miscellaneous; as a thinker I was born at the wrong time and bred in the wrong way. I like to hope that someone may later revive parts of my philosophy in more favorable circumstances. Yet for my own happiness I was philosophical enough. In a commonplace psyche I kept alive a spark of pure spirit which cast an impartial light, as far as it could reach, over the *universitas rerum*. This light cannot be blamed for the quality of the objects it found to shine upon: nor can it be taxed with inconstancy for shining only spasmodically, since that is the fault of the psyche and of the world in which it was formed. Pure spirit is no complete being: only a capacity to feel and to think upon occasion. Its light must be subdued to the quality of the things it touches. Yet in touching anything, no matter how foul, the light itself is not contaminated. In my various books I have discussed things at very unequal removes from the fountain of spirit within me. But that center was truly philosophical. I can identify my self heartily with nothing in me except with the flame of spirit itself. Therefore the truest picture of my inmost being would show none of the features of my person, and nothing of the background of my life. It would show only the light of understanding that burned within me and, as far as it could, consumed and purified all the rest.

AMERICANISM

THE MODERN WORLD is founded on two principles contrary to nature: that money is prolific, and that the useful is the good. This system multiplies without limit the needs and the servitude of the people; destroys all leisure for the soul; withdraws from regulation for human purposes those materials which the arts are to transform; imposes on man the breathless rhythm of the machine and the acceleration proper to precipitated matter; applies an inhuman measure to human action, and gives it a truly diabolical direction: because the end of all this delirium is to prevent man from remembering God.

THESE ARE THE WORDS of Jacques Maritain, a contemporary philosopher who exercises a marked influence in intellectual circles: yet they must sound strange and archaic to most ears. Can anything existent be contrary to nature? And except perhaps for some preacher rekindling the embers of emotion, what can be the use of talking about "remembering God"? Nevertheless, for the few who can lend to Maritain's words their intended definite meanings, these words may seem to be full of concentrated

21

wisdom. Modern civilization has an immense momentum, not only physically irresistible but morally and socially dominant in the press, politics, and literature of the liberal classes; yet the voice of a dispossessed and forlorn orthodoxy, prophesying evil, cannot be silenced, and what renders that voice the more disquieting is that it can no longer be understood. When the prophets or apologists of the modern world attempt to refute those vaticinations, they altogether miss fire, because of their incapacity to conceive what they attack; and even in the exposition of their own case they are terribly confused and divided. It is seldom indeed that their conscience or their thoughts have passed over entirely to the side of their action.

Let me attempt to formulate what our reply to Maritain might be, if we could do justice to his position and understand our own.

The ancients saw and imagined everything on the human scale. For them the terms of thought were obvious and unquestioned: either gross physical objects, with their observable habits, or else the categories and the passions of the human mind, as grammar or poetry might distinguish them. As for the unknown, they conceived it mythologically, by projecting into nature and enlarging to a divine scale these same human terms, and peopling the infinite with optical images, verbal powers, and invisible persons. What wonder if they felt at home, and thought they had discerned the true face of reality, by inspection in the foreground and by divination beyond? A man had but to open his eyes, and whet a little his natural understanding, and when once a few childish cobwebs or tears had been wiped away, the truth of things would luminously appear. If there was ever a conflict of dogmas under such circumstances, it could be only incidentally, when some confusion or diseased doubt had arisen by chance, or at the instigation of some wicked demon. That difficulty once solved, or that temptation vanquished, the philosopher could settle down again contentedly in the conscious possession of the truth.

Not that the classic sage needed to claim omniscience, or more than a relative and human rightness in his pictorial knowledge. But this qualified rightness was sufficient. Let God, he could say humbly, let the angels and demons watch over their several spheres. It is the part of man to cultivate his arts and purify his spirit. The arts proper to man were precisely those which, directly or indirectly, redounded to his spiritual benefit. Being on the human scale, these arts could be mastered and digested humanly, practiced openly, and piously transmitted and learned. Their products could shine with the infused beauty of labor and of love. The same impulses and powers that had given form to the work could afterwards contemplate it with joy and inward understanding. Everything reinforced and clarified humanity in man, and the non-human encircling mystery was masked as decently as possible in archaic symbols, expressing the various attitudes which human prudence must needs assume towards the inevitable or the unknown.

If Adam and Eve could have brought up their progeny in Eden, mankind would have needed no other system of philosophy than that of the ancients. But sorrow knows better; in the wilderness migration was pressing, war imminent, labor exasperated, and henceforth intellectual innocence and clearness were things not only difficult to attain but foolish to preserve. There were hints of horrible mysteries and perversities lurking beneath the surface of nature, in earthquakes, pests, and conflagrations, in deformed births, madness, death, and the mutual hatred and slaughter inseparable from life. Nature herself seemed secretly unnatural: her true order was alien and hidden, and not what the eye and heart of man had first supposed it to be. And to the world's unhomeliness a great division and unrest corresponded in the mind. Had mankind been now invited back to paradise, they would no longer have known what paradise to choose. How find happiness in peace, if we love danger? How be content with intellectual light, if we crave the darkness of power? Thus insoluble puzzles in things, and an infinite dissatisfaction in the soul joined in breaking down the classical harmony of the universe, innocently constructed on the human scale.

The first break, however, was not away from humanism. On the contrary, it led to a penitential contraction and concentration of the natural prospect, on lines more strictly moral and logical than ever. Almost at the same time all over the world, the Hebrew prophets, Socrates and Plato, the Indian and Chinese philosophers, transformed mythology and interpreted it in a new moral or spiritual sense. Its original office of dramatizing the round of nature, or magically assisting it, was suppressed, and the gods, or the forces of nature, were conceived as spirit-

ual powers, guardians of personal or national virtue. What
had been a garden became a fortress and a church. There
was a desperate retrenchment of the spirit upon its home
defenses, all else being declared essentially subordinate or
relatively unreal. Another life or other lives for the soul
were elaborately prophesied, so as to hearten and direct
supernaturally the pilgrim spirit toiling through this world.
Religion, as we know religion, became the center and the
explanation of everything.

The course of religion, however, has never run smooth.
To the innocent superficiality of thinking on the human
scale, it adds the artifice of twisting the natural course of
things into a moral fable. The wonder is that so many
religions have been able to maintain or to recover something of their influence through so many ages. Founders
or reformers of religion are necessarily exceptional men,
men over whom moral faith and metaphysical imagination
hold absolute sway. They very naturally impress and convince a few other exceptional souls; but if their teaching
spreads widely over mankind, it must needs be greatly
diluted and counteracted by all the instincts and insights
of the old Adam. Religion for the majority can never be
anything but a somnolent custom or an uncomfortable
incubus. Practical disloyalty to it fills all the free moments of life; murmurs and jests against it are pervasive in
society, even in the so-called ages of faith; and open re-
bellion is always smouldering in the sly intellect and the
young heart.

An official door actually remained ajar even in human
orthodoxy into inhuman regions. Astrology, alchemy, and

magic might be questionable pursuits morally, but nobody questioned that physically a field existed which these arts might explore darkly. From the beginning mythology had scarcely disguised the monstrous or grotesque secrets of nature under dramatic masks; and the earliest philosophers had sketched naturalistic (and therefore inhuman) systems of the universe, still pictorial in their terms, but already infinite, impersonal, and aimless in their movement. Even Platonism and Christianity, in their demonology, recognized that under-working spirits might fill the air, and might be enticed or exorcised by appropriate rites.

Through this trap-door our modern experimental sciences have entered the stage; and it is important to notice their initial relation to the pictorial cosmology, naturalistic or religious, which previously filled the scene. It was never the possibility of magic sciences, or the truth of a kind attainable in them, that orthodoxy denied; but the pursuit of such knowledge was deprecated as morally dangerous, because such knowledge was tricky and insecure in itself, fed evil passions, and alienated the soul from her proper virtues, from her domestic affections, her eloquence, her religion. But the age in which the modern arts were launched upon their surprising career was not interested in those sanctified things; on the contrary, it had grown heartily sick of them, and hankered instead after strange knowledge, cheap riches, and troubled pleasures: it ached to pillage and to explore. It was the age of Doctor Faustus. Doctor Faustus was a learned man, but impatient, embittered, and lustful; full of contempt for that silly orthodox intellect, always thinking on the human scale. How much grander, if less edifying, were the real secrets of nature! He was not afraid of burning his fingers, nor of the devil; he was an intellectual busybody, mousing about among incipient impossible insights. He felt that there are profound unimaginable depths in nature, from which indefinite stores of energy might be drawn, if we could only hit on the right formulas and ceremonies. He did not hope for light: he was willing to potter about for ever, floundering among absurdities; but he hoped for power. He was the forerunner of Bacon and of the pragmatists.

The event has proved that Doctor Faustus, like Columbus, was not misled by his instinct for discovery. Nature truly has hidden depths, and if these depths are skilfully tapped, or if they shift of their own accord, all the surface may be transformed. Those grubbing alchemists and declaiming magicians were true prophets in principle: it was hardly their fault if they were still humanists and conceived the future triumphs of the arts in terms of a gorgeous and sensual omnipotence. They could not foresee that nature was pregnant with a metallic birth: had they foreseen it, we need not doubt that, after a moment of pained surprise, they would have heartily acquiesced. Romantic aspiration and impatience would be false to themselves if they did not readily accept the result of their own revolts. The fundamental motive is the thirst for change, and a belief that a happy change is possible. Experience must be transformed, enriched, freed from its present predicaments. If the next phase in the world's history turns out to be metallic, what of that? We have only to become a little more metallic ourselves, and indeed we are bound to do so. An age of mechanism will tend to alter the rate and quality of the passions in us, if not of the senses; ambition will turn in the direction in which it finds satisfaction possible, and the mechanic and the airman will feel a happy thrill in living in a world made of taut wire. Even in the old days, most people were perfectly content not to be poets or saints, and to live by a current code of morals somewhat different from the one preached to them in church. The mechanized democrat has merely learned to have the courage of his real convictions, and to laugh at all that retrospective snobbery about being cultured and refined, a scholar and a gentleman. He is amply sustained by social contagion and approval, by rivalry, by keenness to perform any chosen task, and if possible to break some record; also by a sense of technical mastery in controlling the unimaginable souls of his machines, even if it be in sport only and for no further purpose. Moreover, he escapes many of the old torments and vices of mankind: his animal passions are muted by publicity and business, no less than his liberal thoughts. He cannot be cruel to his motors, as he might have been to his beasts of burden; and the instinct for success and co-operation renders him a friend to his associates, where personal pride, or even ideal enthusiasms, would have made him a mortal enemy in his heart to almost everybody. He claims, or ought to claim if he was consistent, no proprietary rights over his female companions, as if he were an old-fashioned husband or lover. He feels a certain comfort and dignity in his private self, isolated and undistinguished as he is in the million. If ever a sudden instinctive sympathy breaks through this

isolation, he may even know a frank and complete friend-
ship, natural to detached equals; a free bond which had
been rendered impossible by the feudal entanglements of
Christian society and religion. His romantic impulse is
therefore not likely to die out, as if a mechanized existence
could have no zest. On the contrary, as the ethos of Christendom fades more and more completely from the world,
we may expect invention, competition, and organization,
in labor and in sport, to grow always more keen, and to
become more and more frankly their own excuse for
being.

A special circumstance has made it easier for these principles to be accepted theoretically, at least in America, and
to be turned into a national philosophy. Americans as a
rule are tough in action, but tender in mind; their own
secret philosophy might not have been popular among
them, if it had been expressed in brutal materialistic terms.
Even in Nietzsche, romantic materialism needed to be disguised by an idealistic vocabulary and a prophetic afflatus:
you felt "uplift" as you were let down. This could happen, because the ambition of Doctor Faustus or of Francis
Bacon, to transform human life by dominating matter, had
never monopolized the public mind. A religious tradition
and a metaphysical passion existed also. The worldliness of
the Renaissance had been crossed by a wave of Puritan
severity and mystical piety. Protestantism, by making private experience and private judgment the supreme court
of appeal, had embarked upon a second reassertion of
humanism: the newly discovered mechanical world might
be as inhuman as it chose; it could never forfeit its

moral function of being a trial and provocation for the human conscience; and the Stoic hygiene of the mind would suffice to disinfect that alien world, or to render its very horror inspiriting. Moreover, philosophical criticism of knowledge was ready to vindicate human ascendancy over the universe in a new and marvelous way, by reducing the universe not, indeed, to a human scale, but to a human locus. For according to idealistic or strictly empirical principles nothing open to a mind can possibly exist except within that mind, and by its consent or contrivance. Thus a second and truly invincible concentration and retrenchment of man's moral being reduced the spirit to a point, to the invisible ego or consciousness to which any world claiming recognition must appear. The ground was thereby admirably prepared for any philosopher trained in the Protestant tradition to become, if he liked, a worshiper of pure process. The old ark of salvation might be broken up without fear of the deluge, and the whole menagerie of more or less tamed human passions and the keeper, human reason, might be cheerfully committed to the waves; for you were assured that the flood itself was simply your spirit thinking, and unraveling its destiny according to your own secretly omnipotent will. Materialism in life or in science and a complete absorption in mechanical arts could thus prove perfectly congenial to the idealist: they were merely one phase in the development of freedom. He finds these tasks before him because in the unconscious he has secretly chosen and loved them. How simple and exhilarating the prospect before us, if there were really no universe except this rambling experience itself, unfolding its coils according to some free principle of absolute spontaneity, and turning, as it goes, in whatever direction it chooses; never condemned to remember the past, except as a point of departure, nor to foresee the future, beyond the work in hand!

II

Such seems to be, when viewed from the inside, that amiable philosophy of invention which Maritain finds diabolical. As proclaimed in America, where it is naturally most at home, it may be said to rest on two principles: first, a romantic transcendentalism, which views existence as a spontaneous moral adventure; and second, a pragmatic or instrumental conception of knowledge, which declares that the conditions of success in this adventure can be determined only by the very experiment which has transformed them. "There is a moving whole of interacting parts; a center emerges wherever there is an effort to change them in a particular direction." Spontaneous impulses, blowing as they list through a social world, thus provide at each moment the purposes and the standards requisite for progress. "Desires, affections, preferences, needs, and interests at least exist in human experiences; they are characteristic of it." We find ourselves inevitably, by virtue of that transcendental romanticism which is our first principle, in an essentially moral, though perhaps unconscious, world: the enterprise of life, with all its cares, is the *substance* of the universe. But in the exercise of our spontaneity we have now discovered our other first principle, namely, that the pictorial world of the ancients, drawn on the human scale, was all moonshine; that knowledge is *knowledge* only in so far as it enables us to change things according to our desires; and that such knowledge exists only in the mechanical arts. Without experimental verification or fitness ideas are not knowledge, but simply ideas. They may arise, as dreams arise, out of the decoction of past experiences; but they have no other than this vegetative quality and visionary status; they remain (in both senses of the word) immaterial. They are the dead leaves, not the tentacles of life. Even the tentacles (I mean the mechanical arts) are not similar to the controlling forces which they engage or appropriate: and the accompanying true knowledge is but a twist given to the original sensibility of the organism, when those forces are drawn into the vortex of human action and bent to the services of human interests. Such knowledge grafts the mind, through the applied sciences, upon the world of action; and at the same time it humanizes that world by filling it with artificial objects and improvements.

This philosophy combines idealism with practicality in a way obviously congenial to the American temper. Technically, however, the combination might seem to be affected paradoxically, in that the idealism or moralism concerns the *substance* or *ground* of events, according to the Faustian maxim that in the beginning was the Deed: while on the other hand the tests of rightness in thought and in action are thoroughly materialistic. Wouldn't it be more natural to put the material element at the bottom and at the origin of things, as in the systems of the early Greeks, and to leave the idealism for the ultimate harmonies, and the moral perspectives, which the mind might eventually find in that cosmos, or introduce into it? But no: spirit, and the whole moral life, would then be essentially idle, aristocratic, and contemplative—in a word, utterly un-American: and it is too late in the day for the spirit to be that. In the modern world spirit must work for its living or else, on Darwinian principles, it will be quietly eliminated. And what other position, save that of a primary energy, should a working spirit occupy, whose goal must be to master, transform, and enjoy a material world? And what shall the material world, in its turn, claim to be, except the chosen theme of the spirit that creates and transforms it? Even before the days of industrialism, wasn't this the burden of German idealism? We are still in the laboratory of Doctor Faustus. Cosmic brain-storms have settled down to the analysis of matter, and the manufacture of Homunculus, or the mechanical man.

Nevertheless, indications are not lacking that this super-position of material labors on spiritual freedom might be reversed, simply by tracing the implications of this very philosophy of enterprise; and we might be brought back to the classic conception of spiritual freedom superposed upon material labors. Experimental science and the arts which enshrine it, being instrumental, admittedly debouch on something else, which is ultimate; let us call it immediate experience. In this immediate experience the elements must be found that are to have a positive worth in themselves. Some satisfaction, confidence, and clearness will saturate daily life, and will constitute what (if carpers would allow) we might call a modicum of happiness. Happiness is not final in the temporal sense of having no sequel. On the contrary, the happy man is probably more energetic and better fitted to make his further action felt than is the invalid or the wretch. Yet happiness is ultimate *morally;* a sequence of efforts and achievements would evidently have no intrinsic value, and at best be only useful, unless it were pervaded in some measure by incidental pleasures and by a general reflective satisfaction in the life one is leading. It seems, therefore, to be simply a historical accident if at present the American philosopher finds his rewarding work chiefly or exclusively in experimental sciences and mechanical arts. These pursuits involve intrinsic values, in that he probably carries them on joyously and enthusiastically, unless he is too tired; and an eventual change in his interests might any day cause him to subordinate these particular activities to others, perhaps of a religious, political, or poetic sort. The transcendental spirit is nothing if not free: it may easily cease to be addressed exclusively to operations on matter, or to the abstract sciences that define the method of inventive arts.

If we renounced transcendental idealism and acknowledged the natural superposition of experience on nature, we should be merely awakening from the Satanic dream that we were creators and not creatures. Nature is the moving ground of experience and experience a play of moral counterpoint or conscious cross-lights upon the surface of nature. That we are creatures and not creators follows from the fact that we are born to die, are dependent on matter for our very existence, and are addressed in all our passions to our transitory fortunes in the material world. Such recognition of our animal status—no less obvious in our moral than in our physical being—would not compel us to abandon the transcendental point of view where this is in place, namely, in the survey of the world by any particular mind, with its special organs, from its special station, and in its special interests. We might still carry with us a relative incidental, portable transcendentalism, like a field-glass slung on our backs, to focus our observations and guide our wanderings. But the region swept, no less than the interests subserved, would be frankly natural and variable; there would be no insolent claim to monopoly in giving direction to progress, no cheap—and how groundless!—airs of superiority to the past, no ignorant assumption that the tendency which we happen to obey at home, and for the moment, must be the central and victorious tendency in all mankind everywhere. Some respect might be shown for the living soul: each temperament and each philosophy might be suffered to speak for itself. For instance, the possibility of abolishing all this modern business of industrialism, mechanical arts, and experimental science would not be excluded. Some day, no doubt, these things will be abandoned, since they are luxuries, and require a compulsory devotion in mankind at large to rather inhuman pursuits. Yet if, for instance, India should now attempt to restore human life to its ancient simplicity, and to renounce industrialism, it might easily be overrun and subjugated by the iron hand of some neighbor less devoted to spiritual goods: or if they were left alone materially, they might subsist unregarded, as ancient life actually subsists today in the West in a few monasteries and sacred preserves surviving by insulation. We may safely assume, I think, that for the present civilization must continue to become increasingly mechanical.

III

Does this mean that Americanism must spread throughout the world? Yes and no: the equipment, the machinery, something of the manners developed in America will have to be adopted wherever a lively participation in the movement of affairs is desired. But this external participation in methods may only be accepted in self-defense, as they say the Japanese have accepted the Western arts. Something no doubt will be changed in the ancient soul by her new armor; but the explicit aim is to turn the modern arts into a defense for the ancient spirit. Quite in the same way, has not the City of the Vatican installed and set up two conspicuous poles for radio-telegraphy, almost as high as the cross of Saint Peter's?

Here I come at last to what seems to be the distinctive quality, the unshared essence, of Americanism as America breeds it. It consists in combining unity in work with liberty of spirit. There are plenty of sectarians in the United States, plenty of fanatics, propagandists, and dogmatists; but the American absorption in work—a work controlled and directed by the momentum and equilibrium of its total movement—causes all these theoretical passions to remain sporadic, private, harmless, and impotent. Their social effects cancel and disinfect one another; they count and modify the balance of action in so far as they are forms of business; in so far as they are definite ideas they evaporate in loud steam. If the Pope speaks through the radio, everybody listens and thinks that, after all, the old gentleman must be a good fellow; but nobody notices what he says. All that is not business is left free, because it is profoundly indifferent—a safety-valve and holiday folly for those who like it. In America, where all else is precision and hurry, the very speech of the people, when it is more than a business code for co-ordinating action, becomes languid and vacuous; it drawls, it becomes indirect, humorous, and playful, it renounces all responsibility, like whistling, and is not particularly interested in anything or even in itself. Why should this happen in a nation otherwise so lively, and so shrewd in practical perception? Because speech and thought, for the man of action, lag behind the automatic decision by which his action is determined; he sees, he aims, and he hits the mark. Why should he trouble, after that, to express the fact simply in words, to focus description on the truth, or to trouble about what anything is exactly? For him speech and thought are essentially superfluous, belated, pathetic: if he must talk or think, he will take to amiable banter, as if he were fooling with a child: and his work over, the wake of his thoughts will be like those soapy patterns left wavering in the sea-water by the impetuous churning of the screws.

Isn't this looseness in everything in so far as it may not be useful, this blankness of will in respect to ultimates, an evident application of the principles of liberalism dominant in the nineteenth century? No doubt this liberalism retained some part of the enthusiasm for liberty, for breaking chains, which had inspired Rousseau and Fichte; but these philosophers were no prophets of machinery, nor of any sort of material progress. They looked rather to a return to nature, or to patriarchal austerity; they expected mankind, once freed, to become ecstatic and heroic. In the liberalism of the industrial era this sense of being stifled under an alien incubus had largely disappeared. The object was less to snatch liberty by revolution than to profit by it in commerce and to concede it by legislation in all indifferent matters, so as to secure the largest possible co-operation of the public in the work of material progress. Religion in particular was to be made private and optional: so too, if liberalism had been consistent, would have been nationality, marriage, family life, higher education, and all other moral traditions. Property, on the contrary, was sacred, being a requisite stimulus and test for industrial proficiency. A common-school education, too, might need to be compulsory, in order to instil into the entire community capacity for initiative, love of work, optimism, and respect for success. Thus liberalism was tolerant of everything except indifference to material well-being, either in oneself or in others. It favored the accumulation of wealth; Big Business must be highly organized, and requires Big Brains at the top. On the other hand, wealth must not stagnate in a few hands, as if there were any public advantage in princely fortunes or princely ways. The millionaire must remain a man of business, an object of emulation, and an example of success in work.

If nepotism or routine crept into the management of affairs, ruin would not be far off. The state must be addressed to Business, and Business must be managed by Brains. Wealth must circulate and be widely diffused; and if once the standard of material well-being is high enough, all else will be spontaneously added by the goddess of liberty.

What would be the state of morals and culture if these principles had been thoroughly applied? The question is speculative, because the revolution in England and America, and even the French one, only scotched the snake: powerful ecclesiastical, aristocratic, financial, and academic traditions survived, to indoctrinate the public mind, and keep up the standards of humanism. In America especially the English common law, English literature, and British philosophy remained an active ferment; yet in many ways these pervasive influences, while alien to industrialism and to experimental science, were not unsympathetic to Americanism. They, too, combined confidence in practice with anarchy in theory; they tended to foster co-operation in work with independence of spirit. Moral and intellectual anarchy did not, however, become at all alarming. There was not life or energy enough in radical minds to destroy the ruling conventions, maintained by inertia, by custom, and by that respectability without which no Business would be firmly established. And such heresy as there was, lest a killing vacuum should form around it, soon became a nucleus of orthodoxy in its own corner, warmed by the hot eloquence of a few enthusiasts.

Americanism allows that laissez-faire in moral life which it denies in commerce and industry. Not, of course, that it officially tolerates burglars, murderers, forgers, or adulterers. Legal morality still adheres to the general code of Christendom: but all religions, and therefore all theoretical codes of morals, were to be equally tolerated. The question at once arises, how long, if all moral codes are tolerated, those who hold those views can be restrained from putting them in practice. And what authority can the dominant morality retain? Evidently none: yet it is wonderful how long it has taken the liberal world to discover that it has deliberately abandoned mankind to moral anarchy. It has been only in recent years that the Russian revolution, Madame Caillaux, D. H. Lawrence, and André Gide have openly and conscientiously written down robbery, murder, adultery, and sodomy among the inalienable rights of man.

We are still in the liberal world, not at all alarmed by a moral chaos, if only a mechanical industrial order, firmly advancing beneath, renders that moral chaos harmless and entertaining. Or rather—since this vanity of the moral order renders it, for a puritan utilitarian mind, essentially *im*moral—no moral life is countenanced at all save the moral life involved in the very discipline and service of mechanism. Americanism might become a more definite and unified regimen than that which I have defined: the freedom of spirit in it might be surrendered to unity in work. Freedom would then subsist, or be recoverable, only in the orthodox manner, by a voluntary conformity with fate. Every impulse not involved in the common task would have to be killed off; and the so-called freedom that survived would be only that of whole-hearted service. The romantic indetermination of the course to be taken by events would allow us to imagine, somewhat ambiguously, that we personally initiated a part of that mighty movement by which we were irresistibly borne along. Americanism in this case would drop the ingredient, still discernible there, of somewhat lax English liberty, and would conform instead to the German ideal of always living in a thorough unison with the Zeitgeist. This ideal unites thorough social discipline with complete moral anarchy. Everyone is expected to obey, at each moment, the passing inspiration of the national Will: but since that Will has no natural ground and is itself the ground of everything else, its successive phases come as they happen to come. No revulsion of feeling can be perverse, no ambition illegitimate. Indeed, as Hegel says, all the phases of existence will be mad, reason being manifested meantime in the necessary instability of everything.

As yet, however, America is full of mitigations of Americanism. There are survivals; there are revolts; there is a certain hesitation in the main current itself, carrying the nation towards actions and sentiments not altogether congruous with experimental progress. For instance, intervention in the last war can only be very partially interpreted as an expression of Americanism. If freedom of spirit was more characteristic of the British and French than of the Germans, unity in work was more characteristic of the Germans than of the British or French. If we translate the Eternal Feminine of Goethe into experimental physical terms, and call it a tempting passivity in matter, obedient in all directions to an infinitely plastic will, we may actually identify the American trust in work and experiment with German romanticism. Both are equally hostile to any fixity in human morals, in institutions, or in ideas. The punctilio that would stick at violating an old treaty or at practicing on occasion a little surgical ruthlessness, seems from a cosmic point of view a ridiculous weakness. Yet it was precisely this weakness, this punctilio, together with a distaste for the Juggernaut car of coarse idealism, that was finally able to turn the American mechanism against the German, to the serious derangement of the latter. What remains doubtful is whether the two mechanisms, somewhat re-adjusted, will not survive and perhaps merge, while the weakness, the punctilio, and the distaste disappear. Will man throw the reins on the neck of his iron horse, or will he lead it by the halter to the domestic stable, there to be fed on judicious rations, and brought out for labor or sport only when natural human virtues, rooted independently in the soul, require such an instrument?

It is all a question of recognizing, obeying, and saving the human soul. Whenever the flux of matter is organized into an animal life, a relatively permanent and self-preserving soul comes into existence. This animal soul or psyche is a center of organization and moral direction for the body of that creature and for all his arts. Did he cease for a moment, under the contagion of ambient influences or of his own vicious habits, to defend his peculiar life, and to subjugate the surrounding world as far as possible to his own native rhythms and moral uses, he would be committing suicide—a sort of slow suicide by radiation, by the dissolution of his living unity and inner life. The test of rationality in his actions is that they should tend to liberate the native potentialities of *that* soul, and render *that* life more perfect after its own kind. Such perfection is compatible with growth, being the measure and the standard of it: and it is compatible with variety and true freedom in the realm of spirit. As human perfection is not identical physically in the two sexes, or at all ages, or in all races, so it will not be identical morally under all circumstances. The point is that in each of its forms life should remain vital, perfect, and appropriate. It should be *vital*, that is, fed by sap rising from its hereditary root, spontaneously, gladly, freely. A life should also be *perfect*, that is, harmonious with itself, and culminating in a distinct form or order in which all the parts are included without being distorted. Finally, life should be *appropriate;* that is, capable of maintaining itself and feeding on its surroundings, by adopting for its vitality a type of perfection which circumstances render possible at that particular time and place. If vitality were lacking, the soul would dissolve into its parts, perhaps with little souls of their own, and would miss that spiritual actuality which comes of synthesis. There would be intellectual and moral nullity, as in inorganic matter. If harmony were not attained, any synthesis attempted would remain painful and strained: there would be distraction and torment, and a worse fate than unconsciousness. And the same would happen if, in spite of

43

some inner unity, the soul found all her needs unprovided for and all her hopes vain, on account of the maladaptation of her structure to her circumstances. Yet this need of communion and adjustment outwards goes no farther than is requisite to preserve the two internal conditions of a good life, namely, harmony and vitality. The soul therefore always remains master in the moral sphere: obliged perhaps to bide her time and to lie low during some horrible deluge, but never receiving direction save from her own nature.

The relation of a soul to bodily life and to action in the world may be expressed in two ways: first, critically and materialistically, by saying that when an organism arises and exercises self-preserving functions a sensitive and perhaps intelligent soul is found to animate it; and second, dramatically or mythologically, by saying that when a soul of some specific sort descends into matter she organizes that portion of matter in a way consonant with her native powers. The two ways, for a moralist, terminate in the same fact: that for the human soul there is a spiritual life possible, but conditioned by the sort of commerce which the soul carries on with the body and with the world. That this spiritual life—meaning the entire conscious fruition of existence in perception, feeling, and thought—is the seat and judge of all values I take to be an axiom: every maxim, every institution, and the whole universe itself, must be tested morally by its effect on the spirit. The merits of Americanism, and the direction in which we should wish it to develop, therefore hang exclusively on the sort of spiritual life which it may foster.

How does unity in work affect the spirit? And how does freedom of spirit affect it?

IV

American unity in work has a peculiar and perhaps temporary character, due to the great opportunities and rewards which work of the experimental industrial sort has found in the new world. The moral value of this kind of work is one question: the moral value of unity in work of any kind is another question, and more speculative. As to the first, what could appeal more to the virgin mind, or be more exciting, than to explore and pillage a virgin universe? And what could be more artful and slyly victorious than to enlist that universe, like a domesticated animal, in the service of human comfort? And what could be more stimulating to intelligence than this successful labor? But here a glance at the actual state of modern society (of which America exhibits the unalloyed essence) may well check the flow of our reasoning. Enterprising, busy, competent, certainly; happy in work, perhaps; enlightened intellectually by that competence and that science? Hardly. Fed and liberated in mind so that the other half of Americanism, freedom of spirit, may be nobly enjoyed? Certainly not.

I know that the distinctively American philosophy, pragmatism or instrumentalism, warms to the praise of experimental science, and even asserts that there is no other sort of valid knowledge. This opinion is itself symptomatic. The word "knowledge" (like the word "truth," sometimes used by pragmatists as if synonymous with "knowledge") is commonly a eulogistic word; and if all other intellectual possessions save strictly experimental science are denied the title of knowledge, we may suspect that, even if admitted as forms of feeling or of poetry, they will be rather despised. Yet before experimental science had made much progress, perception, familiarity, and insight, on the human scale and in pictorial and dramatic terms, had richly furnished the mind, and sufficed to guide it pertinently in all indispensable matters. All the mechanical arts which experiment has created are luxuries, luxuries in which the poor are now compelled to indulge, instead of in their ancient luxuries, such as religion, story-telling, piping, ribaldry, dancing, and fine holiday clothes. Doubtless those legends and sports kept them scientifically ignorant and unprogressive. Yet considered intellectually, or as furniture for the mind, the artificial abstractions which modern science substitutes for the natural symbols of the senses and fancy have no greater value. They are not truth substituted for illusion, but one language substituted for another. And what a language! Essentially vacant, thin, dark, and unintelligible, it has only one merit: it is a vehicle of power—of power, I mean, over matter. For the purposes of dealing with the flux of matter, far removed in its dynamic texture from the human scale, this experimental and mathematical science is alone relevant: the old arts were only customs, and treated natural things almost as if they were persons, and the sailor steered his ship as if he were driving a horse. When that rude acquaintance gave out, the prayers, oracles, and incantations of the classic mind were nothing to the purpose. The essential darkness of modern science goes naturally with its utility: how should matter not be dark to spirit? A pragmatic knowledge of it is knowledge enough. Such knowledge contains the most expeditious methods of doing business, with the greatest safety and the least possible expense of thought. After business is dispatched (or while it is carried on, if such doubleness does not involve too much distraction) the mind is free to enjoy the sensations, the vistas, the hopes which its contacts with nature are capable of arousing. If geography, history, letters, and worldly wisdom are no longer called "knowledge," they are not absolutely forbidden to survive: they remain a part of experience, idle in so far as not useful in material work, but admissible, perhaps, as by-play and recreation.

Here we may observe that unity in work, in the American as in all other systems, tends to impose unity of spirit. There is a lot of spirit in Americanism, so much that it threatens to overwhelm that liberty and looseness of mind which have hitherto been conjoined with it. If the simple and fearless American admires and trusts the vast momentum of modern business, he does so because his soul shares that momentum. The mechanized democrat is full of hope and assurance, and as far as his imagination can go, he is full of kindness: it is always in physical action that comradeship is most hearty: as you rise from action to thought—especially to original and emotional thought —sympathy becomes more nebulous: it requires the material force of eloquence or ritual words to rekindle it to flame. The whole strength of modern enthusiasm comes from its open or secret sympathy with matter. It cries against material poverty or suffering; it relies on the force of numbers; it foretells irresistible material revolutions: and it dreams of the euphoria of a universal material health. This matter is undoubtedly alive, and if the soul which animates this body prospers within, nothing could be more satisfactory. Nature would have realized here one form of perfection. Yet the human purpose and spiritual sanction must be kept paramount throughout and the question may be raised at any moment whether this mechanical adventure has not unhinged the human mind from its vital animal frame, and imposed on it a mad impersonal ambition. The greatest external success may easily involve an essential failure. The success, being physical, might go on indefinitely; but what if the moral failure should pervade the experiment?

The ancient association of man with nature was on the human scale as in agriculture, architecture, ship-building, and sea-faring; it was filial, brotherly, poetic, even perhaps religious. The disasters involved might occasionally be terrible, but they were incidental. Peace could return; the young will could spontaneously begin its labors anew, as it would its wooing; and the domination of reason might soon be partially reasserted in the arts. But when the miner began to dig deep into the bowels of the earth, in order to feed some smoking furnace with fuel; or when the alchemist began really to transform matter, and the chemist to analyze it down to almost vanishing elements, then something unholy mingled with their zeal. They no longer followed the rhythm of the seasons in their labor, or even that of day and night. Avidity drove them on un-relentingly, until perhaps they dropped exhausted, their natural passions faded away, religion became unnecessary and foreign, speech telegraphic, humor trivial and thin, and the whole mind quick and dry, like a ticking clock. They acquired a kind of expert knowledge; but the effect of habitually thinking only in imageless technical terms was to reduce the mind to a set of signals: and perhaps he who increases knowledge of this sort only increases sorrow, by increasing the material commitments and bur-dens of life, without increasing its spiritual fruits. And this is not the worst. Mechanical art and abstract science avowedly terminate in objects and transformations on the human scale, open to direct experience. But these terminal objects and transformations, the actual experience which the thoroughly mechanized mind enjoys and morally pos-sesses, become themselves poor and childish in the extreme. A man may be tired of being an instrument, but he is not trained to be anything else. In his leisure, any sort of sensual or emotional pabulum will do for him; he wants simply to relax into whatever pleasure is cheapest, silliest, and most good-natured. He reads the modern newspaper and goes to the cinema. It seems as if science which is merely useful and work which is thoroughly economic were bound to end in an experience which is wholly mean.

Union in work has been imposed before in hunting and fighting communities, at least in the intermittent phases of their more intense activities; but this was under the pressure of circumstances, making such union imperative; and a vague and despised freedom to muse as one liked might be allowed to fill up the idle intervals. Many of the notes of romantic poetry and philosophy seem echoes of that barbarous age. Union in work has also existed in more special circles, religious or military, as almost down to our own day in the English aristocracy. Union in such cases was expected to flow naturally from an underlying identity of taste, breeding and capacity. It was essentially an army of sporting leaders, winning its battles on the playing fields of Eton. Something of this kind, *mutatis mutandis*, might be found in the older genteel America, with its honorable hereditary merchants and capitalists, whose achievements culminated in public-spirited foundations and after-dinner speeches. But this society had no liberty of spirit at the top, among the efficient. Spiritual liberty—how incomplete and halting!—was relegated to the second-rate men who served the storm-troops of progress in the mild capacity of clergymen or teachers: their office was to study and to praise the spirit of their betters, and to transmit it to the next generation. Independence of mind, or moral initiative, appeared, if at all, only ineffectually, in the third-rate quasi-foreign ragtag of Bohemian poets and artists and stray intellectuals, whom the law tolerated but whom society surrounded by a freezing vacuum. In a word, where there is union in work, unless this union express a native identity of temper in everybody, liberty —meaning endless diversity—of spirit is dead or dying. At best there can be only that inner liberty which even a Jesuit may enjoy, if his heart can expand to the utmost limit under the accepted discipline. Unless an identical moral nature and set of possibilities are common to all the individuals concerned, unity in work can be nothing but slavery.

V

There is a sense in which man, in so far as he is not adapted to the matter which affects his well-being, must always be the slave of that matter. Indeed, if we defined matter functionally and morally, and called it *the butt of action*, or *the sum of all dynamic and possibly conflicting agencies in the world*, it would follow that union in work was always desirable on the plane of matter. This, I think, is the secret of American strength and American competence. But the plane of matter, while it is that on which survival must be determined, is not that on which the value of what survives can be judged. Moreover, any material equilibrium is always imperfect and precarious because, as Spinoza says, the force of the universe infinitely exceeds the force of any one part of it, such as man or a human society. Integrity can seldom be established in a single man, much less in a community; and the rebellious elements, each with a will of its own, never cease to sulk, to shift their ground, or to break away altogether and set up a rival order on their own account. Criminal these treasons and heresies will be called by the conscience of the dominant organism, as long as that conscience survives; and any lover of form, however impartial he may be, must regret that anarchy which allows incompatible movements to collide inopportunely, and to defeat every possible harmony. Yet inwardly considered, and in their vital origin, the marplots are innocent enough; they are perhaps wonderfully brave; a formative impulse of a new sort is active within them, and causes them to detest and seek to destroy the overruling force, physical or moral, which hopes to suppress them. The tears of the historian should never turn to wrath.

Americanism at first was itself revolutionary, and it still strives to throw off, as useless parasites and impediments, all the older traditions of mankind. But it has become itself a tradition: it has developed a soul that would impose itself on human nature, and remake all human souls in its own image. It is the function of any soul to gather up matter into a living body, with all the radiating arts, and all the spiritual lights which such arts and such a life may kindle. It would be a perfect abdication and idolatry for any soul to forget her own function and to yield instead to the deadly fascination which the general mechanism of the universe may sometimes exercise on the senses and on the automatic habits of the body. The general cataract of nature or of history is, for any soul, only a monstrous and all-devouring chaos. What irony there would be in having learned to control matter, if we thereby forgot the purposes of the soul in controlling it, and disowned the natural furniture of the mind, our senses, fancy, and pictorial knowledge! The greater part of human life, by a biological necessity, must always be carried on in terms of sense, passion, and language. The contribution of experimental science and industrial invention would be useful if it were incorporated in a life of reason adequate to the whole powers of the soul: it would be fatal if it succeeded in monopolizing reason, and substituted blind work for free imagination. We know the impulses that come to the surface in such a mechanized mind, and make up human experience. They are boyish impulses, a series of wagers, and acrobatic marvels, and playful whims. Nothing ulterior of any consequence results from the performance; when a trick in the game is won or lost, you are simply made ready for the next trick. Your soul is vulgarized; you become a clown when you are not a dullard; and the unofficial holiday sides of your nature, when they break through, break through without dignity, order, or formed habits of expression. It is from such a condition that mankind emerged when, in remote antiquity, it began to be civilized. The change came not by studying matter, but by so acting towards it that one no longer needed to study it. The arts had been established in such a way that the practice of them was intelligent and the fruits agreeable. Mankind has now acquired, as it were, new senses, or a new telescopic and microscopic range of attack upon matter: this is a new and better instrument with which to operate. But the purpose must remain the same. If Doctor Faustus, in view of the wonders of nature open to experiment, sold his soul to the devil, he is not forbidden, when the secret is out, to cheat the devil who had morally cheated him, and to repent. Perhaps America, more innocently misled than that old reprobate, may more quickly turn to repentance.

THE SEARCH FOR
THE TRUE PLATO

TIME HAS BEEN exceptionally generous to Plato. None of his works are lost, and his fame and influence seem to be undiminished after twenty-three centuries. Such vogue, however, could hardly be maintained, in a world so inconstant as ours, by a philosophy not possessing an extraordinary adaptability and involving a certain vagueness. A severe and explicit system, however true, could hardly have appealed to people of such different mind and caliber as were the Platonists of various ages. Plato had the advantage of presenting a philosophy which in its first principles was practical and rational—the philosophy of Socrates—but of presenting it in a brilliant literary form and of escaping from it into eloquent flights of fancy, by which it was relieved of its natural severity and made to appeal to mystical and enthusiastic minds. Platonism is accordingly a many-sided and elusive thing, on which each successive disciple impresses his own stamp and grafts his own intuitions. All sorts of things have passed for Platonism, and passed for it with about equal right—Pythagorean

54

metaphysics, academic scepticism, Neo-Platonic mysticism, Christian theology, transcendental idealism, and the mere incoherent practice of speculation, whenever it is warm and rhapsodical.

While the philosophers have been content to adopt and adapt Plato in these ways to their own uses, we should naturally expect historical critics in our own day to attempt an impartial reconstruction of Plato's philosophy as it may have existed in his own mind. Such a reconstruction is rendered exceedingly difficult by the fact, proved both by internal and external evidence, that Plato's works, although all extant, do not adequately cover his philosophy. The authenticity of many of the dialogues is doubtful, and the order in which they were written is a further point which critics feel called upon to settle, although it might seem to be in itself a matter of some indifference; the discussion of it might serve to produce doctors of philosophy at the universities, but might appear to involve no further benefit. Only, in Plato's case, the order of composition acquires a special interest, when we observe that there are notable divergencies among the dialogues in style and in thought, if not absolute contradictions in doctrine. One set is mythological, playful, and humane, another technical, abstruse, and rationalistic. As we give priority to one set of dialogues or to the other, we conceive one of the greatest of philosophers to have moved, as his thought and experience matured (for Plato was one of those philosophers who actually had experience) in one of two opposite directions. The question thus assumes some historic importance and some dramatic interest; it might even be thought to involve an argument from authority in favor of the attitude finally assumed by so illustrious and comprehensive a genius.

While the intrinsic value of the various dialogues remains untouched by such a problem, our notion of their living author is profoundly transformed as we shake our historical kaleidoscope and let those luminous fragments of his mind fall together into one pattern or another. Was Plato a conscientious scholar, did he subject himself to a scholastic discipline, working over abstruse technical problems, in order to rise afterwards, when his apprenticeship was over, to a poetic treatment of real things? Did he shake himself loose from dialectical scruples in his maturity, and proceed to handle the deepest themes with the freedom and irony of a master?

Such is the view that has commonly prevailed. If it has not been insisted upon with more emphasis, the reason is that such a view tends of itself to make people careless about those works which are conceived to be merely preparatory, so that these works come to be practically ignored. The ordinary practice, even among scholars and philosophers, is not to read the *Laws* or the *Sophist* at all, and to glide over the *Parmenides* as an anomalous and singular performance, possibly not really Plato's. Yet the *Laws* is the longest, one of the latest, and the most earnest and unequivocal of Plato's works. The *Sophist* is one of the most incisive and the *Parmenides* one of the most profound. By losing sight of these dialogues, however, the question of their relation to the rest can be passed over in silence, and Plato can be considered as if he were the author only of the more poetic and interesting pieces.

Or, if we take the other view, was Plato by natural inclination a poet, and did he, by the inspiration of his genius, turn at once the ethical doctrine of Socrates into a metaphysical idealism—the expression of his youthful and enthusiastic intuitions? Did he later analyze and interpret these intuitions in a more critical and sober way? Did he study the problems which they called up and reduce his theories more and more to mere expressions for practical and moral realities, until at last, in the *Laws*, all allegory and hypostasis were abandoned in favor of a literal definition of spiritual goods—the very thing which all that idealistic machinery had from the first been meant to express and to glorify?

Some such view, or at least the chronological theory which might support it, has recommended itself to many detached scholars in recent years. To speak only of those who write in English, Professor Lewis Campbell and Dr. Henry Jackson some time ago made suggestions tending to a reconstruction of Plato's philosophy. Professor Campbell's chronological theory, being buried in the introduction to an edition of the *Sophist* and *Politicus*, attracted little attention. Dr. Jackson's papers were more noticed. But the very strong chronological argument they contain, based on a minute analysis of the group of critical dialogues, was prejudiced by a general interpretation of Platonism which was based upon them; and the learned public, generally feeling that interpretation to be unsympathetic and forced, condemned also the chronology which had been used to introduce it. These English views, uttered by their distinguished authors only, so to speak, in an academic whisper, have recently been trumpeted by Mr. Lutoslawski in his scholarly and readable book, *The Logic of Plato*. Here they are supported by a verbal apparatus which, if not calculated to convince the obdurate, serves at least to give the new conception a certain emphasis and to call attention to the more solid grounds which support it, grounds which Mr. Lutoslawski's analysis of the growing Platonic logic brings convincingly before the reader.

The most distinctive feature of his book, however, is the attempt to find a purely linguistic and mechanical method for solving the question of chronology at issue. As not only the style but also the vocabulary differ notably in the various dialogues, it has occurred to Mr. Lutoslawski, as to some of his German forerunners, to make statistics of Platonic language, showing in tables how often every word which seems characteristic of the latest Platonic style, as exemplified by the *Laws*, occurs in the other works. Thus, all the dialogues can be arranged in a series according to their linguistic affinity to the *Laws;* and we are to infer that this series will correspond to the order of composition. This method, of course, might be more exhaustively applied, if a greater number of words were counted and compared. The results already attained lead unequivocally to the conclusion that the logical dialogues are later than the poetical, since their language has a much more marked resemblance to that of the *Laws*.

If further research should confirm this result, we should have, according to Mr. Lutoslawski, a scientific key to the order in which Plato wrote his works.

Such an argument is open to serious objection. Without denying the striking variety of Plato's compositions, it may be doubted whether the change in style is due to a permanent change in the man, and not rather to different and reversible poses in the writer. It is natural to use a different vocabulary in dealing with a different subject. For so imaginative and dramatic a genius as Plato, it is particularly natural to hold various moods and interests in suspense, and to give utterance to them in turn without being obliged to concentrate, for the convenience of future critics, all the poetry in one period of one's life and all the logic in another. Doubtless verbal tricks and incidental phrases, being comparatively unconscious and instinctive, may serve as indications of certain epochs in a man's literary life. But here, too, much allowance must be made for the power of imagination to carry its own atmosphere with it, so that revulsion to a mood or subject belonging to a buried stratum of the mind may rejuvenate and resurrect a whole vocabulary and gamut of sentiment which had fallen into disuse and been overlaid by other habits. If second childhood can refurbish so many faded ideas, it is because the brain is a miser and hides more treasures than it is often willing to spend. There is no difficulty, therefore, in conceiving that Plato should have tapped his various interests at various times and more or less adapted his expression to each theme he took up.

Critics too often forget that a great writer may have

great elasticity, and if any performance seems to them essentially new or at all incongruous with a previous one they take refuge in the easy hypothesis of a forgery. Who knows how many of his works Shakespeare or Goethe, Cervantes or Byron could be suffered to retain under the restriction of never saying anything different in tone from what he had said before! Plato was a great artist, a great observer, a haughty though amiable judge of all opinions. He knew the limitations of art and the often ambiguous complexities of dialectic. What more conceivable, therefore, than that he should have sometimes etched a subject and sometimes filled it in with the richest colors, sometimes followed up the logic of a problem, and sometimes that of a passion? In the *Parmenides*, indeed, we have these extreme phases actually juxtaposed—a singularly picturesque scene, scintillating with brilliant and profound ideas, being followed by a singularly abstruse exercise in dialectic. But both parts are in substance and manner appropriate to their theme and worthy of their author.

Mr. Lutoslawski takes the *Laws* as the starting point of his verbal investigation. That choice is unobjectionable but not inevitable. We know on as good authority that the *Timæus* is also a late work, and the unfinished *Critias* was actually at Plato's death in process of composition. Now the *Critias* is a humane and highly mythical fragment, written in an excellent style, perfectly congruous with the *Republic* and *Timæus*, with which it was intended to form a trilogy. The *Timæus* is the most wildly mythical of all Plato's writings, exceeding in fancifulness and arbitrary complexity even the *Symposium* and the

Phædrus. There is no doubt, therefore, that Plato towards the end of his life was able to write well, and willing to compose myths in which the gods and the ideas appear as metaphysical existences. We should not on that account reverse Mr. Lutoslawski's chronology and revert to the notion that the logical dialogues are all early. Too many details, apart from mere matters of language, forbid that conclusion. If the great mythical trilogy—*Republic, Timæus,* and *Critias*—is unfinished, so is the contrasted logical tetralogy—*Theætetus, Sophist, Statesman,* and *Philosopher;* the last a dialogue announced in the others but never actually written. Death, which we are told surprised Plato pen in hand, seems to have interrupted both these opposed methods of expressing his philosophy. It would not appear that the two trains of thought were distinctly divided in time nor, to their author's mind, contrary in tendency.

A further circumstance, strangely neglected in these discussions, shows that Plato, towards the end of his life, was driving all his horses abreast. The *Laws,* admittedly the product of his old age, shows a phase of thought equally distant from the mythical and from the logical, so that whichever of the latter two we place last, it will have to synchronize with something wholly alien to it in character. The *Laws* is a monument of didactic formalism, a sort of prolonged catechism, dry, unadorned, and uncritical. It would seem to show a mind disenchanted with poetry, contemptuous of dialectic, careless of eloquence, and bent solely on vindicating antique manners and the antique gods. Had the other works of Plato's old age been lost to us, what an opportunity there would have been here for the constructive critics, who insist on making every one evolve through a series of successive phases and react like a vegetable on the changing seasons! We should have been told that the Plato who wrote the *Laws* had passed into his dotage, had reverted to the impressions of his earliest years, before he ever knew Socrates, and had become a stern and reactionary bigot. Philosophy and literary luster had forsaken him altogether and given place to a Spartan severity and Roman-like piety. Since he was always averse to the evident currents of life in his age and country, it would have been argued that he was alienated at last from his own genius, in which he may have discovered too many affinities with a corrupt and vapid civilization. But, as it happens, the author of the *Laws* was simultaneously writing the *Critias*, a work of pure and delightful imagination, a mythical echo of the glories of Athens. And if Mr. Lutoslawski and those he represents are not mistaken, he was engaged at about the same time upon a series of analytic discussions which should straighten out the misunderstandings involved in a too poetical rationalism. If such contrasts are admittedly found in the same period, and if the *Parmenides* unites equal contrasts within its own compass, what hope can there be of deciding, with any precision, in what order the other dialogues were composed, or of classing them in watertight chronological compartments?

The phases of Plato's thought need critical co-ordination, but little would be accomplished towards that end by arranging the dialogues in a temporal sequence. Even if we accept Mr. Lutoslawski's arrangement of them, we need not infer from it either a change in the author's fundamental views, whatever they may have been, or an improvement in them in case they really developed. Mr. Lutoslawski, like Dr. Jackson, shows that a more acceptable and rational logic is contained in the critical dialogues than in the poetical; but how could it have been otherwise? It was not when Plato gave free rein to his imagination and spoke in parables that his conceptions could bear literal analysis: what they needed then was imaginative and sympathetic interpretation. But when he undertook to think accurately and incisively, as in the *Parmenides, Philebus* or *Sophist*, we may reasonably take him at his word. The order in which these investigations followed one another, if they were not contemporary, does not alter their intrinsic quality. Not even the philosopher's own preference for one kind of speculation over the other can change their respective functions or prevent their possible harmony. We may ourselves reasonably waver in our preference, and adhere now to the *Phædrus*, for instance, for its ideal inspiration, and now to the *Parmenides* for its critical acumen. The only source of contradiction lies in the critic's want of literary judgment and of a reasonable latitude in interpretation, so that he insists on gathering scientific truths from dithyrambics and figs from the cedars of Lebanon.

The merit of Mr. Lutoslawski's classification seems to us to be that, either by accident or by the secret influence of a philosophic idea, he has grouped the dialogues in a way to make clear their internal logical relation to one another. They fall into four groups of which one presents the philosophy of Socrates and the others expand that philosophy in three different ways. The first group consists of the charming little pieces, with the *Apology* at their head, in which Socrates' person is faithfully portrayed, and thoughts are expressed which do not go beyond the characteristic scope and genius of that master. In the second group, which may be best represented by the *Republic,* Socrates is still the speaker, and many a lifelike trait puts him now and then visibly before us. But the thought, although Socratic at bottom, is given a great extension both in conception and in expression. It is inconceivable that the philosophy of government, of art, of love, or of immortality which these dialogues contain should ever have been framed by Socrates. Yet in each case Socrates' utilitarian rationalism is the key to the Platonic mysteries which have overlaid it. We shall never understand Plato's idealism, here so eloquently developed, if we forget that his "Ideas" are Socrates' definable moral functions, and his "good," Socrates' principle of benefit. The mythical and metaphysical expression of these Ideas, however, is carried so far that Plato might well have felt, we should suppose, the impropriety of attributing his ideal constructions to Socrates. But he seems to have been himself more conscious of their Socratic basis than of their non-Socratic extension. These thoughts were after all what Socrates might have arrived at without self-contradiction if he had been a poet and an enthusiast. The import of this ideal philosophy is still exclusively moral and humane; all that the world has since taken for supernatural physics was merely poetic metaphor.

In the last two groups, however, Socrates no longer appears, or appears in a subordinate position, as the object of victorious though respectful criticism. The third group, which contains the critical dialogues we have already mentioned, is devoted to correcting the misunderstandings incidental to metaphysics in general and to the mythical idealism of the second group of dialogues in particular. We are taught to think accurately, to remember what we are thinking about, and to recognize the relativity of all the categories of our thought, especially of the One and the Many, which were then playing so important a part in the controversies of the school. Neither in the *Parmenides* nor in the *Sophist* and *Statesman* are the Ideas abandoned; far from it. But they are explained, and we are warned of the danger they run of becoming irrelevant if they are made absolute.

The fourth group, in other indirect ways, further illustrates the ideal philosophy. Socrates had left nature out of account and declared that physical reality was not an appropriate object for science. Plato fully accepted this doctrine, as he is careful to tell us at the beginning of his pseudo-physical treatise—the *Timæus*. Another great master, Parmenides, for whom Plato had almost as much veneration as for Socrates, had taught him the same lesson and had given him a similar example by beginning his physics with the warning that he was now entering the field of unreality, illusion, and merely verbal play. Nevertheless

Plato, like Parmenides himself, was attracted by the legitimate desire to be complete, and not to leave our notions of nature and the gods, as Socrates had done, to chance and to tradition. He therefore wished to write a philosophy of nature. But instead of composing it, after the manner of the naturalists, out of phenomenal laws and empirical observations, he had the brilliant idea of writing the history of the universe in the inverse order, and from the point of departure of nature's moral functions, of what Emerson would have called nature's commodity. The project was to give an imaginative description of cosmic evolution, each phase showing a stage in the expression or emergence of ideal values, of those very things in which a Socratic philosophy might take a legitimate interest. Utilitarianism, which had led Socrates to renounce natural science, was thus made the principle of a new and inverted natural philosophy. The cosmology of the *Timæus* is a vast parable. The creation is described from the point of view of the moral values which it was to generate. These alone could make nature interesting or comprehensible to the moralist. In despair of discovering her causes, he described her justifications. The length of the intestines, for instance, was to be explained not by some hypothetical natural cause, but by its ulterior service to human happiness and virtue. The intestines are long, Plato informs us, to free man from the bestial necessity of spending his whole life in eating, and to give him leisure for philosophy.

This jest, by dint of repetition, soon ceased to seem one, and, together with the similar "jeux d'esprit" which fill the

Timæus, ended in that prodigious misunderstanding of final causes from which the world has not yet emerged. The study of functions, to see how things might conduce to human life and happiness, led to the habit of explaining the things by the functions they happened to have; and this ideal principle of explanation was then represented as a principle of genesis and growth. Man came at last to the absurd idea that organs can be produced by their own functions and things by their own effects. What had been the glory of Socratic ethics, the study of functions and of the values things have for man, became the disgrace of Aristotle's physics and the bane of all subsequent philosophy.

History was to have been treated by Plato in the same spirit. In the *Critias* he was to furnish a mythical picture of the origin of civilization, obtained by protecting its ideal into past time. The state which in the *Republic* was constructed laboriously and conscientiously, by considering at every point what would be ideally best, was now to be revealed in a fable, feigning to describe the original constitution of Athens. But, at the same time, lest the pictorial elements in such a myth should make us forget the practical and serious kernel of the whole, the *Laws* hastened to provide us with a set of enactments, showing how concrete and rational would be the actual embodiment of that supernal principle of good in whose honor we had all along been philosophizing. For what these speculative dreams circle about is the ideal philosophy itself, that legitimate extension of Socrates' wisdom which fills the second and noblest group of Platonic dialogues. It is morality touched with imagination and applied to all the interests of a liberal life. The fabulous way in which these intuitions are put before us has contributed to their acceptance, but has led at the same time to their misinterpretation. Indeed the misunderstanding was essential to their diffusion, for philosophy never becomes popular until it is believed to offer a logical defense for current prejudices.

The idea of good or of excellence is scientifically defined by Plato as the fulfilment of function; but this fulfilment is illustrated by an elaborate picture of an ideal state—a Utopia in which much else is conspicuous besides the exemplification of justice. Love, too, is nobly defined as the attraction to the good and beautiful everywhere; but this rational sublimation of the passion seems, in his account, to involve the abandonment of all its real objects in favor of some celestial shibboleth, some absolute focus of incompatible perfections. Immortality is also philosophically conceived as the soul's natural affinity to the eternal, and assimilation with it; but this rational immortality is mythically represented by fables about transmigration in and out of subterranean and celestial abodes. Finally, the preformation of the categories, the native predisposition of the mind to certain forms of conception, is analytically proved, and the reality of Ideas is inferred from their necessary function as objects of thought; but this transcendental and rational philosophy, too, is compromised by its mythical expression, and we seem to be informed about material existences in the upper heavens, standing about like statues to be admired by passers-by, and inspected by the soul before she descends to this world from that celestial museum.

Now, in each of these cases, Plato's doctrine if taken ideally and morally is profoundly true, but if taken materially is clearly fabulous. He is expressing the values and ideas of real life in mythical form and in the guise of Utopias and of personified abstractions. This situation should have been made clear by the least thought about the original functional character of these Ideas, even if Plato had not composed critical writings in order to warn us that in the others he was speaking in parables. Yet so great is the power of images, that very power against which Plato's rationalism was directed, and so slight the power of reason, that tradition has turned that most intellectual of thinkers into a mystic, and that keenest and mellowest of critics into a blundering mage. There is hardly a piece of sentimentality, theosophy, or mystification that has not sought to cover itself with his name. That is the price Plato has paid for having clothed his speculations in poetry and for having thereby appealed to a public very much less intelligent than himself. Some thinkers, like Spinoza or Fichte, are saved by their severity from a degrading popularity, or if they achieve it for a moment are soon superseded in public estimation by others who, like Hegel, have the art of seeming to be conciliatory and of comforting those public illusions which they secretly despise. Plato's charms were in this way the most serious enemies of his better intuitions. We may even suspect that his condescension to popular weakness was at the same

time a sop thrown to his own natural inclinations, and
that he allowed himself at moments to be overcome by his
own fancy and to yield a half ironical belief to the very
myths he was consciously inventing to express a rational
philosophy. It is hard, in reading certain passages in the
Phædo and *Timæus*, not to attribute to them a prophetic
intention, as if the author would gladly have been accepted as an inspired oracle whose words had a sacramen-
tal value and whose visions revealed supernatural truths.
In pagan times it did not seem impossible to touch divinity
either through one's dreams or through one's virtues. Only
a few years later Alexander could be proclaimed a son of
Zeus. It is not inconceivable that in Plato's case, too, pride
should have played into the hands of superstition. Such
sibylline charlatanism may seem inconsistent with that
Socratic candor and enlightenment with which Plato is
permeated; yet in this masterful genius much that was un-
Socratic both underlay and overlay the Socratic discipline,
and we must not be too much alarmed by glints and sparks
of mysterious influences and esoteric pretensions. In this
soul's career, a winged horse of mythology added itself to
the two steeds which reason, the Socratic charioteer, had
already to struggle with, and brought the chariot into as
great danger of accident as did the refractory, sensual
yoke-fellow of virtue. With the joltings and deviations of
a course followed under so many conflicting impulses, we
can never be quite sure that we have discovered the intended goal, or that any single goal was pursued with
absolute constancy.

The exact balance and doctrinal outcome of Plato's

philosophy, not being formulated in his writings, must necessarily escape us. In a remarkable passage in the *Phædrus*, which no critic of Plato should forget, he disparages the power of writing to communicate the truth. A book, he tells us, can answer no questions, give no explanations, correct no misunderstandings. It cannot enter, as the philosophic guide should, into the learner's mind, to draw from its own depths the implications and potentialities of the argument. A Socratic and conversational method is the only guarantee of genuine comprehension and rational conviction. A book is a dead oracle, reiterating with stupid persistency the same words to every fresh inquiry; a book can never re-apply a principle, or reconsider an assumption, and is therefore the most unphilosophical of things.

This idea, put with exquisite dramatic propriety into the mouth of Socrates, who wrote nothing, is no less characteristic of Plato himself, for all his brilliant and prolix compositions. In every department of his genius and life, there seems to have been a spontaneous rush of imagination curbed and mastered by the iron hand of reason. It is said that in his youth he wrote tragedies and other poems, a pursuit from which he was weaned by the sobering influence of Socrates. The story may be apocryphal, but it well expresses, in an apologue, the inner history, as we may fancy it, of the man's whole soul; the artistic impulse bubbling up, and the dialectic conscience supervening; the pride, the eloquence, the love of beauty, and the sensuous fancies of an Athenian dilettante, all hushed and overawed by the sense of impending social disaster, by logic, by conscience, and by the memory of ancient gods. Such a contrast and conflict is visible, as we have seen, in Plato's writings; but there is every reason to believe that could we see the man as he actually was and compare his discourses and aspect in the Academy with the works we now possess, the conflict and contrast would be much more striking. He was more antique, both in his severities and in his indulgences, than we should like to imagine. Possibly if we could see him as he was in his later years, we should think him a semi-Oriental sage, filled like a new Pythagoras with echoes of sibylline traditions, both Hellenic and barbarian, and like a second Parmenides, absolutely dogmatic and convinced of his supersensible knowledge. At any rate there are sides of his character and conviction which we half see, but can hardly do justice to: for instance, his ancestral religion, his admiration for Sparta and for Egypt, his mathematics, and his apparent surrender to Pythagorean speculation. No one can tell how much these things may have modified in real life the temper and standards of a man who in his writings is generally so urbane, so liberal, and so rationalistic. Much less can we be sure that other influences which escape us altogether were not at work in his mind.

His personality, whatever it may have been, has passed with his country into the irrevocable flux of all that is phenomenal. We should be unworthy of the best lesson that Greece and Plato can teach us if we regretted their disappearance too much. It is not the idiosyncrasies of that man or nation that should interest us most, but rather the truth, excellence, and beauty, wherever found, which they first clearly envisaged. If it were still in Plato's power to tell us more about himself, it is very doubtful whether he would consent to do so. Could he now re-write or supplement his works, so as to make them perfectly unequivocal; could he affix dates to them and add footnotes and excursuses, we may well believe that he would refuse with scorn to minister in that way to our curiosity and vain erudition. The truth, he might say, cannot enter the mind passively through the eyes, whether they gaze on the sights of the moving world or pore over the pages of a classic. As the body cannot be strengthened by another man's exercise, so the mind can gain understanding only by its own dialectic. The most important questions which a book raises are questions which a man must answer for himself.

THE ETHICAL DOCTRINE
OF SPINOZA

SPINOZA AS A MORALIST holds a peculiar position. He does not belong to that class of writers whose purpose is rather to eulogize virtue than to explain it; nor to that other class which takes delight in pointing out the weaknesses of human nature, and loves wit and piquancy better than complete truth. Both these schools write for effect, although in different ways; one is pre-occupied with the practical tendencies and the other with the brilliancy of its writings; neither is satisfied with a plain statement of the facts of life. In disinterestedness, in the absence of an ulterior practical motive to color his inquiry, Spinoza resembles the Epicurean moralists; and in fact in its homely, week-day application, his doctrine might pass for that of a cautious Epicurean. But the source of Spinoza's inspiration, his master thought, is the complete negation of the Epicurean ideal. The Epicurean lays all the stress on his surroundings and manner of life; for him a beautiful and comfortable environment is what makes life worth living. But Spinoza makes no mention of such things; it is the significance of the world and not its pleasantness that makes life worth living to him.

There is not, however, in Spinoza any native insensibility to aesthetic and intellectual pleasures; one does not feel that Spinoza is a Philistine; for, strangely enough, Philistines when they try to philosophize, are apt to become Epicureans, although ideally this system is the most contrary to their nature, since it consists in treating life as a fine art. Spinoza's ability to appreciate the finer things of life is what makes his subordination of them impressive. Any fanatic can abuse the Epicurean ideal and declare that there is but one thing needful; but the earnestness of such a man is apt to lose its force when we consider that he is incapable of appreciating more than one ideal. Spinoza, to be sure, was not a broad-minded man, he was not a man of intelligent sympathies; on the contrary, his thinking all turns in very narrow circles about its center. But at the same time his master-thought is of such a nature that it makes anything like fanaticism impossible. For this master-thought is nothing less than the divine right of the real, before which all ideas alike lose their authority. The sum of reality, the one terrible unavoidable presence, was alone to be reverenced; respect for the fact, worship of the inevitable is the fundamental thought of Spinoza.

We hear much about a possible religion of science; Spinoza has one ready for us. The scientific spirit—allegiance to the fact—becomes in Spinoza one with the spirit of worship. That all things happen by a uniform law, that a thing can be understood only by knowing its cause, that the highest good is the unification of knowledge, that reason desires only what is necessary and acquiesces only in what is true—these are principles as essential to Spinoza's religion as they are to science. It is strange, indeed, that Spinoza is not more generally hailed as the prophet of the new dispensation; perhaps the cause of this neglect of him is that the scientific spirit has not yet penetrated into all the thought of scientific men; when they sigh for the religion of science, they are dreaming of a religion founded on facts, which shall retain all the Christian ideals. When Spinoza therefore proposes to them to dethrone the Christian ideals, to give the facts not only labor and love but acquiescence and worship, they think it is a hard saying, and walk no more with him.

After all, it is a great sacrifice that Spinoza asks us to make when he would have us confess that our approvals and disapprovals are nothing but personal equations; or at most, indications of the needs and interests of the human race. Somehow it gives a man a sense of dignity and self-satisfaction to believe that his interests are those of the universe and his likes and dislikes those of God; but this faith Spinoza would have us abandon. A doctrine which bids us lay down our lives and gives us, meantime, the assurance that our cause is absolutely just and our adversary's cause absolutely unjust, demands a smaller sacrifice than a doctrine that bids us keep our lives and give up that assurance. We have, indeed, according to Spinoza, a right or even a duty to live and fight against those who have an equal right to fight against us; for thus we all serve the great power that keeps the world in motion; but we must give up the idea that one man rather than another is doing the will of heaven; that one thing rather than another is pleasing to God.

Spinoza's ethical doctrine consists of two distinct parts; he distinguishes them himself, yet without pointing out the very different footing on which they stand, doubtless because in his mind the subordination of one to the other was obvious enough. The first part is a description of the way thoughts and passions arise in the mind. Here we learn that by the eternal necessity of things, a great diversity of opinions and passions arise in men, which are divided by Spinoza into two classes, called adequate and inadequate ideas. An idea with Spinoza is equivalent to what we call a state of consciousness; it is not confined to the mere perception, but includes judgments and emotions, as well as acts of the will. Spinoza, indeed, has good reason to use one word for all these processes, for he believed them to be identical in their nature. Every perception, according to him, involves an act of judgment, nay, is an act of judgment. Our mind is governed by a system of checks; every perception left to itself is a hallucination; every suggestion of an act, left to itself, is the performance of that act. A man has an adequate idea of any object when his consciousness includes the explanation of that object in so far as that object is represented in his idea, for an idea to be adequate need not represent all the details of its object. What it must include is the immediate cause or explanation of what it does represent. To have an adequate idea of a ship I need not have in mind everything the ship contains, it is enough I perceive nothing in it of which I do not understand the construction. There need be no doubt that

77

such is in fact Spinoza's meaning; for no man could have an adequate idea of a triangle if he first had to know all that is involved in its nature. Much less could anyone have an adequate idea of God, who is absolutely all-inclusive. The adequate idea of God which Spinoza claims to have is adequate in so far as it perceives perfectly that God's existence is involved in the existence of anything, and the existence of everything is involved in God's; for adequacy consists in the clearness, not in the fullness of ideas. A man, on the other hand, has an inadequate idea when the proximate cause or explanation of that idea is not in his consciousness. Both adequate and inadequate ideas may involve emotions; if the idea is adequate, Spinoza calls the emotion an activity of the soul, if the idea is inadequate, he calls the emotion a passion.

Here the second part of Spinoza's ethical doctrine begins to appear; he eulogizes one set of emotions by calling them activities, and casts a reproach on others by giving them the name of passions; whereas, in the ordinary use of words, his activities are also passions and his passions are also activities. Spinoza calls the love of knowledge an activity, because it is awakened by something we comprehend, and fear he calls a passion, because it is produced by what we do not understand, and it is significant that he already begins to condemn all emotions which spring from inadequate ideas; description begins to give place to praise and blame. Nevertheless, there is a certain propriety in calling an emotion springing from inadequate ideas a passion, because such an emotion arises partly from causes foreign to the consciousness of the man who feels it; he therefore thinks it more arbitrary and tyrannical than if he were aware of all its causes. On the other hand, if he saw within himself the sufficient reason of that emotion, he would regard himself (and justly, according to Spinoza) as free in regard to that emotion; not, of course, that it was possible he should not have felt it, but that nothing outside his consciousness was required to produce it.

The first part of Spinoza's ethical doctrine consists, as I have said, in a description of the causes of men's emotions and actions. The psychological side of the question does not concern us here, but the great underlying conception is this: All things are equally necessary, and therefore equally reasonable. What men do from inadequate ideas seems to them irrational, because the causes of it lie outside themselves; but in God all ideas are adequate and for him all things are rational. Good and bad are not to be applied to things absolutely. The good is what is favorable to some end, but God acts for no end; the bad is what threatens the survival of some particular thing, but the flux of things is the life of God. We form a certain ideal of human life, and whatever conforms to it we call right, whatever contradicts it we call wrong. There is nothing in things to make them better or worse; the difference is in their relation to us. Our essence is will to live, and on this will alone depends for us the worth of all things.

Here we pass into the second part of Spinoza's moral system—the discussion of the highest good. Nothing can be good for us but what tends to preserve our nature; our nature is preserved only in so far as our adequate ideas have free scope; therefore the only good for us is the possession of adequate ideas. The highest good, the only good for man is to understand.

By means of the conception of the essence of man as consisting of a man's adequate ideas, Spinoza seems to have intended to connect this second part with the first. It is a plausible thing to say that our own survival can be our only good; that the instinct of self-preservation is the source of all our desires. But such a statement is plausible only when we mean by our preservation something very different from the preservation of our essence in Spinoza's sense of the word; when we mean by instinct of self-preservation an instinct to preserve much more than our adequate ideas. Spinoza's presentation of this second part of his doctrine shows that he knew it rested on very different grounds from the purely descriptive part of his system. The claim of adequate ideas to be the highest good consists mainly in the fact that they tend to destroy the passions; but this consideration would appeal only to those who already felt that the passions should be destroyed. Another claim is the intrinsic value of adequate ideas as satisfying our desire for knowledge; but then the desire for knowledge is not always strong. Other arguments in favor of the chosen standard are found in its probable effect on the state and on the character; that is, in its coincidence with other standards already recognized by men. All these arguments in favor of adequate ideas are so many admissions that adequate ideas stand on the same ground as any other thing men are wont to desire, and have no special right to be regarded as the chief good. In fact, I cannot think that Spinoza meant to present in this second portion of his work more than one of those ideals of human life which may become the standards of good and evil; he cannot have pretended that his choice of understanding as the chief good would commend itself to everyone. He explains the arbitrary character of all ideals too plainly and forcibly to assert that his own ideal is not arbitrary. All that he means to do is to describe a type which to him was the most attractive—the type of the man overwhelmed with a sense of the unity and reality of things, the sense of unity contributing a mystical, the sense of reality a scientific element, in short, the man of adequate ideas. The tendency of a man's mind commonly determines what ideal he shall adopt; and if he is strenuous and single-minded, as Spinoza was, he will do much towards realizing that ideal in his own person; therefore we need not be surprised at the strong likeness between Spinoza's ideal and himself. His strenuous and single-minded nature, indeed, makes him present his ideal in a dogmatic way; and it is not impossible that he convinced himself that it followed necessarily from the first part of his system. In fact, his system was worked out to satisfy the demand for adequate ideas and for a single absorbing object of thought. The dependence of the system on this ideal in his own mental history may have been vaguely felt afterwards as a dependence of the ideal on the system. A man worried by a theorizing spirit might take satisfaction in constructing a theory of happiness; but only by a singular limitation of view could he pronounce happiness to consist in the construction of theories.

All that Spinoza advances in support of his ideal is interesting and true so far as it goes. To acquire clear and distinct ideas is often to remove the causes of fear, of hate, and of love. The knowledge that all the suffering in the world is necessary is apt to make a brave man braver, but it also makes a hard-hearted man more hard-hearted. The conviction that right and wrong vary with personal feeling and with the interests of the race must tend to promote tolerance of others' faults; but as it may also promote tolerance of our own, we may doubt whether the interests of the race can make it right to believe a doctrine with such a tendency. Adequate ideas may make me blessed, but I may prefer to be rich; they may even make me immortal, but I may prefer to be merry and to die. Spinoza can, indeed, assure me that the intellectual love of God is a good that affects the mind to the exclusion of all else; I may believe what he says and yet dislike a state of mind which too much resembles monomania. In the end Spinoza must admit that blessedness, like everything else, is not desired because it is good, but is only good when it is desired; and I must be allowed to retain my conviction that adequate ideas are inadequate for life.

Nevertheless, the demand of science and of the whole intellectual side of our nature is for adequate ideas. In his search for them Spinoza arrived at a conception of the world which is unrivaled for sublimity. Nothing can express the feeling of insignificance, of helplessness, which assails one in the presence of Spinoza's God, from the necessity of whose nature infinite things follow in infinite ways. All thoughts of beautiful and ugly, of late and early, of good and bad, fall away from us. We cannot judge the reality that remains; we cannot love it; we can scarcely think it at all. What we bring away is the feeling that all things are equally sacred; that what we love is no better than what we hate, what we blame no worse than what we admire. No system of morals can follow from this insight; we cannot even say that to gain this insight is the moral aim, for those who have it are no better than those who are without it. The only difference which this insight enables us to make between systems of morals is that between the systems by which men unconsciously live and the systems which some men have consciously devised; for here is a difference in reality, the former being combinations of acts and the latter combinations of words. But common men living by any of them or philosophers defending any of them may be alike content with the part they play. No one plays a better. It will still be true that each system has a definite tendency; each will produce a different kind of men; but which kind is admirable depends on which kind is admired. Therefore, as it seems to me, Spinoza is perfectly consistent in developing the practical part of his system to suit himself. In abandoning the absolute point of view he does precisely what the absolute point of view encourages him to do. He keeps the ideal he had before and rejoices in it. The absolute point of view sanctions all pursuits in so far as they are actual; it sanctions none before they appear as actually followed in the world. The search for the absolute point of view is but one pursuit among many, sanctioned by the absolute point of view only in so far as it is actual; for the absolute point of view sees in things only their reality. Spinoza's ideal happened to be the attainment of the absolute point of view; this is also the ideal of science. We all acknowledge that it is desirable to have adequate ideas and to attain the absolute point of view, for we all share the instinct of curiosity. But Spinoza valued this ideal not only for the satisfaction it promised to the enquiring instinct, but mainly because he saw that exclusive attention to the absolute point of view might still the emotions and make a man desire only what is necessary and acquiesce only in what is true. Yet the mere understanding of the absolute point of view, the mere belief that it is final, cannot still the passions unless it is able to arouse opposite emotions. Spinoza's ideal, then, is not so much the possession of adequate ideas as the exclusion of inadequate ones; the engrossment of the mind in its adequate ideas, so that the pleasure of understanding the causes and nature of conscious life may be the only thing in consciousness. This is what he calls the intellectual love of God; and he describes the ideal society as consisting of such institutions as, under the given conditions, will tend to arouse the intellectual love of God in men's minds.

The arbitrary character of this ideal is evident enough; but when I call the ideal arbitrary I do not mean to condemn it; on the contrary, a moralist who confesses that his ideal is arbitrary has a better chance of moving us than one who pretends to speak the oracles of the absolute. The aspirations of men interest us more than their exhortations and we have more respect for the standards which have imposed themselves gradually on human society than for any theory of ethics. Spinoza's ideal, however, seems to us too narrow. In so far as it calls for adequate ideas we share it, for we also like clear thinking and curious knowledge; in so far as it excludes inadequate ideas we reject it, for we are not willing to renounce faith and love, pleasure and ambition.

Aesthetic and social demands must be satisfied as well as intellectual; these call for greater spontaneity and audacity, for greater variety in the objects of pursuit. What is the use of calling one's self free, if one is to do nothing? We prefer to be a little more subject to the influences of the weather, and to enter with more zeal into the life of the day; we prefer to be jostled a little in the crowd to walking alone in the desert. On the other hand, for truth's sake, we would not have the sad things of life ignored any more than we would have the gay things of life despised. To say nothing of more tangible causes of woe, this absolute point of view which Spinoza would have us attain, what does it do but reduce all ideas to hallucinations and all this hurricane of being to an aimless gust? It is very easy to say that in so far as men are rational they desire nothing but what is necessary and acquiesce in nothing but what is true; but this rationality is built on the ruins of our vitality; it means the abandoning of all we love and the dethroning of all we reverence; it is that complete self-surrender which involves death. After all, Spinoza did agree with Plato that wisdom is a meditation of death, for the life which he would have us consider involves the extinction of our separate being. So long as we have anything to live for, so long as we have any concern for what happens to us and to our fellowmen, we cannot acquiesce

85

in what is true and we must desire what is in fact impossible. I believe that the absolute point of view which Spinoza has so impressively, so overpoweringly enforced cannot be avoided; it is the ocean in which every stream of thought is lost; and for that very reason Spinoza's apparent optimism seems to me deceptive. The final word must always be a contradiction of our ideals, of those ideals which alone make things good or bad. The world becomes one oppressive, tyrannous fact, eternally and inexplicably present. It may be possible to lose one's self in this eternal reality, so as no longer to feel its weight: but why should one wish to do so? It is much easier and much saner to confess once for all what seems to be the truth, and then to go about one's other business, guided by the ideal of one's country and of one's heart.

SPENGLER

IT IS ONE of the foibles of romanticism to insist on rewriting history and perpetually publishing new views without new matter. Can we know more about the past than its memorials transmit to us? Evidently we cannot *know* more; in point of truth concerning human history, any tradition is better than any reconstruction. A tradition may be a ruin, broken unrecognizably, or shabbily built over in a jungle of accretions, yet it always retains some nucleus of antiquity; whereas a reconstruction, say a new Life of Jesus, is something fundamentally arbitrary, created by personal fancy, and modern from top to bottom. Such a substitution is no mere mistake; it is a voluntary delusion which romantic egotism positively craves: to rebuild the truth nearer to the heart's desire. Romantic philosophy may still employ the word truth, which has a thrilling sound, like the horn of Hernani; but in retaining the name it disowns the thing, with which it is temperamentally out of humor. The real truth is eternal: you may turn away from it, or you may turn towards it, but you cannot construct it or reconstruct it. Therefore romanticism, when radical, denies the reality of truth, and transfers its name to something else: to the utility, prevalence, vivacity, or internal coherence of ideas, however subjective or pathological. Now such ideas, though probably false, may be stimulating and poetical; and one of the virtues of romanticism is precisely the love of images, of detail, of ironical contrasts, of profusion of reports, of indefinite suggestion; and all this, besides mere glitter, has its value even for the lover of truth. It keeps the mind, as it were, out of doors, facing the exuberance and boundlessness of Nature. Though moodiness and arrogance may be the source of romanticism, its ultimate effect is to reduce the human will and all its wilful imagery to a natural accident: and Nature, for a mind that has passed through romanticism, is no longer the marble cage of a classical economy. She is infinite. The instinct to transcend human egotism and human morality is rational no less than mystical; it is abundantly fed by sober science and reflection; but romantic feeling may render this alien infinity picturesque and humorous in our eyes, and to that extent friendly to a free spirit, rather than crushing.

All these lights and shadows of romanticism seem to reappear in the work of Spengler, the latest and most ponderous of its German prophets. His two thick volumes[1] are swollen with a bewildering variety of alleged facts, insubstantial enough in themselves; for we know nowadays better than a hundred years ago, at the dawn of romantic philosophy and history, how fast the most authoritative academic views change on every subject, how often they contradict one another, and on what slender evidence they

[1] Oswald Spengler, *The Decline of the West.*

are apt to rest. Even if Spengler were a leading professor in each of the branches of learning which he deflowers so sweepingly, we might suspect that there was more fancy than fact in his science. For what is his thesis? That there is a certain order of phases which recur and must recur in the rise and fall of every great society. Spengler does not follow, like Hegel, a thread of true history, interpreting it dialectically and giving it out as alone central or significant: he surveys instead the whole panorama, and creates a sort of botany of events; and this in two stages, one obvious and Linnæan, another more Pythagorean and occult. On the surface, he picks out the brighter flowers from the weedy garden of history, counts their petals, notes their colors, and considers their manner of growth and of going to seed. We are pelted with multitudinous assertions which, poor wights, we have no means of testing; and we are filled, in any case, with that emotion of *Reichtum* and *Fülle* so dear to the German heart. But, attempting to go deeper, Spengler offers us an occult botany as well; for where the form, color, and growth of his flowers are by no means identical, as in Egypt compared with China, or in the Greek world compared with the modern, he nevertheless persuades himself that they exactly correspond, and are *really* forms of the same species. Here is a revival, in respect to history, of that theory of fixed species and eternal *genres* which once found favor in biology and in the arts. As a tragedy, in whatever age or language composed, was required to have five acts and three unities, at the risk of not being a tragedy according to Aristotle, so now every civilization is required to pass through a classical, a magian, a Faust-like, and an imperial phase, at the risk of not being a civilization according to Spengler. Naturally, these necessary phases appear in so many disguises that it is hard to say what, precisely, they may be; but if we compare Spengler with Hegel and with Houston Stewart Chamberlain, who seem to be his next-of-kin, we may observe that his philosophy of history is more impartial. Spengler has more respect for the exotic, and more knowledge of it; he is not content to describe the principal ingredients of a single tradition, Hebraic, Hellenic, Germanic, as if nothing else counted in his snug universe, made to declare the glory of one chosen people or of one chosen idea; he sees in his own times neither the culmination of the world nor its collapse, but a phase in its mutation, such as has often occurred before and may often occur again. Germany and the present age are thus put where they belong in the midst of a flux of events in which they have no pre-eminence. The dogma of progress disappears and, for that very reason, instances of actual and finite progress in specific directions can be honestly traced, when we have taken for the moment the point of view of some living interest. The botanist recognizes his struggling flowers, however widely dispersed and curiously modified; the logician, taking a bird's-eye view of history, thinks he can discern the same patterns endlessly repeated in every part.

Thus the superstition of historical idealism is abandoned, but the illusion of it is retained; and the consequent advantage is not unmixed. The views of Hegel and Chamberlain represent a last revision of Hebraic prophecy: they express the vitality, the faith, the arrogance of a stubborn people struggling against infinite odds: if intellectually preposterous, they are morally powerful or even sublime. In them romanticism at least bravely takes its life in its hands, and rushes to a passionate suicide. In Spengler all this narrow zeal and party-spirit are absent; the idealism which in the others was a war-cry, in him is only a hobby; and we may ask ourselves why, having reformed his national philosophy so far, he could not reform it altogether. I am perhaps no philosopher myself; but I can hardly understand what pleasure anyone can find in wanton extravagance. If various plants or institutions can be traced back materially to a common source, this fact is interesting; and if affinities appear between various forms, even when different in origin, this circumstance is interesting too; but in both cases the divergencies are no less real than the similarities, and all the profit of tracing either the one or the other lies in clarifying and elaborating the picture of each particular thing in its own ideal individuality. A cultivated mind clings as to its natural friends to the salient moments of history, when men were noble and arts perfect; but these moments are rare and traversed inwardly by the most disquieting infections and rumblings of decay. On the other hand, minor beauties, incipient arts, and joyful accidents are scattered broadcast even in the darkest ages and in the most savage lives; the desert has its palms and the moor its heather; the bleakest down breaks here and there into a copse, or slopes into a dale, a rivulet, or a meadow. Why deprive these odd nooks and high stony places of their beautiful singularity? Why say that there are only nine kinds of possible nooks, or only one form of true mountain? The metaphysical pretensions of Spengler's idealism, in seeking to impose a pet pattern on the flux of existence, not only do violence to the incorrigible variety of Nature, but in the effort to conceal their falseness they compromise the purity of the intuitions which they express abusively. Such pretensions may make a system; they may even make a reputation; but are they worthy of a philosophic mind?

The whole force of Spengler's perceptions—and they have sometimes a remarkable force—seems to me to lie in another quarter. It is subjective, moral, lyrical. Like the epic and tragic poets of Greece, we may transport our own passions into the irrevocable past, and give them a nobler expression in that distant setting. We may vivify a slender tradition with a fresh wonder and a new moral; the vivid fiction will have an interest for us quite apart from its historical truth, because poetry, as Aristotle says, is truer than history; that is, it is nearer to the roots of action and estimation in ourselves. Now Spengler's political botany, the tragic pattern which he discovers repeated everywhere, is a help to intuition: it dramatizes the past for our imaginative pleasure. Analogies are the wings of memory; they are seven-league boots by which we may traverse formidable distances, and sweep aside irrelevant details or contrary facts which would only oppress the mind if it could retain them. Intuition, far from penetrating by a miraculous feminine gift to the truth of things distant, falsifies even things present: it substitutes a luminous essence for their obscure diffusion; and dramatic

intuition in particular synthesizes elements never themselves co-existent. A man's view of history is necessarily
personal: it exhibits his politics, and his politics, if genuine,
exhibit his heart. As Plato's *Republic* was avowedly a
means of writing large the economy of the civilized Greek
soul, so any intuitive philosophy of history will be a means
of writing large the sympathies and capacities of the philosopher's mind. In Spengler's case, for instance, we can
easily see that his private studies and his nationality are
responsible for the part assigned to mathematics in his
Only Possible Idea of Culture, as well as for the appearance there of a special Faust-like or musical phase. These
personal notes would offend, if we could seriously regard
such a philosophy as a study of forces actually governing
events; but the same peculiarities become innocent and
even amiable, when we take them for private vistas, tragic
insights of a mind deeply engaged in the very flux which
it thus attempts to dominate poetically; that is, always with
a profound reference to its own loves and its own fate.
The romantic poet crying in the wilderness of history is
then like a Homeric hero telling us how manfully he
vanquished the god Scamander when caught and almost
carried away in that rushing stream.

May we not drop the superstitions or illusions of romanticism and yet catch occasional noble themes recurring
in the confused orchestration of Nature? May not history,
unfalsified, justify epic intuitions of retrospect and prophecy? Undoubtedly: Homer himself is a witness to it, and
every other poet and philosopher who has surveyed the
world without arrogance and without fear. Even others,

93

like Plato and Dante, who were officially pledged to a moralistic view of the world, have often known how to re-translate the fable, and keep and value it in their hearts only for its spiritual meaning. When a man with any depth of soul proclaims a hierarchy of values or sees in events anywhere a supreme culmination and glory, it is evidently no pattern in history or purpose in some god that can compel him to exalt those particular features; he might actually witness their realization, and they might leave him cold, or utterly alienated. That which clothes events with interest, and even endows each of them with its specious unity, is the apprehension of them by the spirit, when they respond to the temper or capacity or secret hopes of some soul; and that imagined event will always seem supreme to a man which is the image of his highest natural good. In this beginning of self-revelation and self-fulfillment lies the true meaning and the whole value of his ranging intuitions.

After reading Spengler, I have observed an instance of this in my own person. Being in Rome, and occasionally entering the Pantheon, I find myself telepathically thanking Spengler for a new insight. Now whenever I stand there I say to myself: This grandeur in unity, this splendor in emptiness, this harmony in silence, this vastness in seclusion—all this is *magian*. This is the first mosque. Dates and derivations may be what you will; you may refer this structure to Etruria and this decoration to Greece; in their marriage here those elements have generated a different, an incomparable beauty. You do not come here, as you might go to a temple or to a church, with busy petitions and anxieties, trying to keep your votive doves quiet in their basket, or troubled in your conscience by that other sweet sin of yours of which you cannot repent. You come here to divest yourself of yourself, as you might leave your sandals at the door. You come to submit and to be disabused, saluting silently a perfection and an immensity which annihilate your life, and yet somehow overwhelmingly renew your secret happiness. How beautiful seems this wholeness, how impertinent those catastrophes rumbling in the distance, which more deeply emphasize this peace! I need only go out into what is ironically called the open to find myself in the midst of congestion, in a frantic world where, to no purpose, all is blowing, whizzing, tooting, scampering, and jostling; yet even in the stress of that lively reality, some humorous consciousness may survive of the quietness beyond. If I have loved things Greek or Gothic or Baroque—and I by no means intend to renounce those loves—was it perhaps only a tender passion, a fancy-love born of a sort of sexual contrast, because my soul was a fascinated stranger in that willful world, and in herself secretly devout and magian? Perhaps those Homeric heroes and those Christian knights, dying beautifully stupid and young in their wanton valor, seemed to me so satisfying only because, without perceiving it, I held a deeper love in reserve: a quiet pleasure in the divine irony by which all things mortal are disinfected and transmuted into their essences, becoming friendly to one another in their diversity and complementary in their lyric charm. The realm of truth is magian like the Pantheon. All things, in the impartial light of eternity, show like marbles inlaid richly but unobtrusively in one seamless dome, windowless like a hollow gourd, yet vertically open to the heavenly air and the perfect blue.

JAMES'S PSYCHOLOGY

THE SAYING OF the Preacher, that to everything there is a season, is easily forgotten when the passions run high. In the time of weeping we feel that no time can really be fit for laughter, but that the very existence of laughter denotes a frivolity and hardness of heart over which we should weep; and in the time of hopeful and enthusiastic building up we feel that a time to break down what we have built has never a right to come. Something of this exclusive and imperious passion seems to belong also to the spirit of an age. Whatever this spirit may be, it tends to pervade everything, and no department of life escapes the influence and contagion of the interest of the hour. Even philosophy, which boasts to be eternal, and is reproached with being unprogressive, succumbs to the fashions; and of late she has made many attempts to dress at least parts of her person in the newest garments of science. Science is now so "easily queen," and has recently contributed so much to human enlightenment and comfort, that nothing could be more natural than such attempts. Especially in psychology is it legitimate to wish to be scientific, and to arrive at conclusions that shall be not merely speculative, but capable of verification and of compelling universal assent. For our minds are parts and products of nature as much as our bodies, and the thoughts and feelings that arise in us are never separated from those physical phenomena which sometimes we call their causes, and sometimes their manifestations. Our cogitations and passions, and still more those of our neighbors, ought, we feel, to be accounted for; and men's humors should be neither more nor less predictable than the weather. It is hard to believe that this nearest and most familiar province of nature, our own lives, should be impossible to survey and comprehend, when such remote and unimagined fields as those of chemistry and astronomy have been mapped out successfully. Nevertheless, in spite of the Germans, there is as yet no science of the mind. There are psychologies in plenty; but it must be confessed that each has its own method and embodies a personal conception of what the facts of mind are and how they are to be studied. There is no body of doctrine, held by all competent persons, that can be set down in a book and called Psychology.

This fact, regrettable as it may be in itself, will persuade the judicious not to grieve that Professor James, while he has written fourteen hundred pages about psychology, has not produced a system of the human mind. His book[1] does not pretend to cover the entire field, or to lay equal stress upon every portion of the subject. It deals with those points in which the author feels a personal interest, either on moral and philosophical grounds, or on account

[1] William James, *The Principles of Psychology.*

of recent experiments and controversies. It is essentially a collection of monographs, and in fact many of the chapters have already appeared in various reviews, in the form of articles. As a textbook the work is at once too incomplete and too voluminous, but as a book to be read and referred to it has every advantage; for by daring to be incomplete it avoids ever being dull and perfunctory, and by daring to be voluminous it succeeds in being exhaustive on several subjects. Indeed, nothing could be more instructive and interesting or, considering the subtlety of the argument in some parts and the minuteness of the detail in others, so wonderfully clear and easy to read. The lively style no doubt contributes to this end. Professor James's manner is so homely and direct, so full of humorous and startling turns, that one seems to listen to an improvisation rather than to read set paragraphs written out in cold blood. But individuality is here more than a charm, more than a human warmth and personal flavor pervading the discussions; it is a safeguard against pretension and hollowness. Those who deal with the abstract and general, who think impersonally and along the lines of a universal system, are almost sure to ignore their own ignorance. They acquire what has been called the architectonic instinct; their conceptions of things are bound to be symmetrical and balanced, and to fit into one another with perfect precision. They fancy they overlook the world; they feel they comprehend every department of nature to which they have given a name. Their cold breath congeals the surface of truth into some system; and on that thin ice they glide merrily over all the chasms in their knowledge.

But Professor James's simplicity and genuineness have saved him from this danger. He is eager for discovery, and conscious that too little is known for any final or comprehensive statements. The result is that in his book more than in many books of philosophy that which is known is set down, and the rest is omitted.

The general reader will probably be most interested in those chapters which have ethical and theological bearings —the chapters on belief, on the theory of conscious automata, on the will, and on necessary truths. The last contains the author's theory of knowledge and is the most interesting perhaps, from the point of view of general philosophy. Necessary truths, like those of mathematics, he tells us, are not results of experience; they are expressions of certain ingrained habits of thought, habits which cannot be revised while human nature remains what it is. That the mind has such a structure and such inevitable ways of thinking is to be accounted for by natural causes, by spontaneous variation, and by selection. The innate and inherited character of these habits and intellectual instincts is no pledge of their infallibility. A mind, to be sure, cannot escape from its own ways of seeing things; these ways of seeing things are its own individuality and essence; but another mind need not have the same structure, and may react differently on the world. There is a front and a back door, as Professor James puts it, through which external influences may reach the mind. The back door is the organic structure of the body, the state of the brain, spontaneous variations in bodily functions, growth, disease, and decay. Our thoughts and feelings, our very necessary truths and primary interests, are dependent on these bodily conditions. To change them is one way of changing our conscious life. The other way is by affecting the senses; this is to enter the mind by the front door. We can properly attribute to experience only that element of consciousness which is furnished by the objects of sense; the rest, and the more important part, is due to the innate structure of the body. In the same spot, animals of different species live different lives and have a different experience. A cat and a dog living in the same house live in different worlds. The same objects surround them, but their interests, habits, and instincts are diverse. In this way we see that, while man is a product of nature, nature has endowed him with a structure, and with mental and practical predispositions; so that our reactions on the world, and even our conceptions of it, are due much more to the sort of brain we are born with than to the sort of objects among which we live.

Professor James tells us that, in all this, he removes himself from the company of the empiricists and joins the ranks of the *a priori* philosophers. But we may be allowed to doubt that he will be welcomed by his new friends or estranged from his old. Few people are now inclined to deny that we inherit a nervous system, and that the quality of our experience depends on what that system is. The cause of quarrel is not so much the origin of our necessary truths as their authority. When empirical thinkers say all knowledge comes from experience, they are not so much denying that there are innate conditions of experience— the organs of sense and the structure of the brain—as they are asserting that our natural axioms and presuppositions have the value of knowledge only by virtue of such application and confirmation as experience gives them. Our ideas may come spontaneously, but only the gradual test of experience can teach us whether they are fit and true. A luxuriant imagination is alike the source of great discoveries and of great illusions; the possibility or impossibility of verification alone can teach us which is which.

It is not from the side of naturalism or empiricism that Professor James need fear attack. All his battles are with a metaphysical psychology. The most striking characteristic of his book is, perhaps, the tendency everywhere to substitute a physiological for a mental explanation of the phenomena of mind. Psychical for him is only the result, the product, the total consciousness of the moment. The machinery by which this is produced and explained, the links by which it is connected with other conscious states, are entirely physical. He will have no mentality behind the mind. In the abstract such a conception is familiar enough. It is held by all the believers in automatism and by all the more avowed materialists. For them, too, a mental state is the direct transcript of its physical conditions; former mental states have nothing to do with it directly. Stop the brain, knock me on the head, and all the momentum and interest of my conscious life are helpless to produce any further consequence. My demonstrations stop, my memory fails, my will lets go its object, and all the effort and labor of my thought lead to nothing. A psychological derivation of any mental fact can, therefore, never describe its true cause. The psychological antecedents could not have produced the result had the physical connection been broken; while this constellation of atoms in the brain, however produced, is bound to give rise to this particular thought and feeling. But Professor James, to whose religious and metaphysical instincts materialism is otherwise so repulsive, has here outdone the materialists themselves. He has applied the principle of the total and immediate dependence of mind on matter to several fields in which we are still accustomed only to metaphysical or psychological hypotheses.

One of these fields is the well-known theory of the association of ideas. For this he substitutes the connection of processes in the brain, and denies that ideas have any existence in the interval between their first and later appearance in the mind, or that they are the same ideas at all when they recur. It has been a habit of philosophers to speak of the association, combination, and persistence of ideas. These expressions, if taken literally, imply that ideas are beings; that they move in and out of the mind like so many personages in a comedy. But where have they been meantime? It may be said they have been stored in the memory; but is the mind a sort of green-room, where ideas gather to await their recall before the footlights of consciousness? One may say so; it is not an unnatural figure of speech. But if we look to the facts rather than to words, we shall hardly believe that ideas exist after they fade from consciousness. Ideas are not substances that exist by themselves and now and then allow us to look upon them. They are creatures of our thought, bubbles of our stream of life, momentary figures in our mental kaleidoscope.

When we lose sight of them they no longer exist. Nothing that may follow them in the mind can really call them back, for they are dead; they cannot hear the prompter or mind their cues, for they are not there. The non-existent cannot be acted upon; it can feel no attraction.

Association is purely a physiological matter. In the brain currents may tend to flow in beaten paths and revive former excitements, because the modified brain actually persists, and retains impressions and predispositions to habitual action. The repetition of a brain process will of course make the idea recur which was first connected with it; but neither the process nor the idea it produces will be absolutely similar to the previous phenomenon; and just as the brain process is only an arbitrarily bounded portion of the total active brain, so the idea will be but an arbitrarily bounded portion of the total consciousness of the moment. In fact, Professor James's conception may, perhaps, be best expressed by saying that the human mind is a series of single sensations, each of which has the whole brain for its cause and the whole world for its object.

A further illustration of this may be found in his striking theory of the emotions. These, according to him, are sensations caused by that motion of the body which we commonly call their expression. Fear is the sensation of trembling, anger the sensation of set teeth and clenched fists, joy the sensation of a bounding heart and expanded bosom. Extraordinary as this reversal of common conceptions may seem, it is really involved in the physiological principles we have been dwelling upon. The thought or perception which, as we say, arouses a passion can do so only indirectly—only because the physical condition that involves the thought leads to the physical condition that involves the passion. So much will hardly be denied by the unprejudiced; and if this concession does not amount to saying, with Professor James, that we do not tremble because we are afraid, but are afraid because we tremble, it amounts at least to this: fear is produced by a state of the brain by which trembling is generally caused also.

The question between Professor James and other modern psychologists is not, then, one of principle; it can only be one of detail. Professor James thinks that the cerebral condition that produces violent passion involves the excitement of the sensory centers; unless we feel the agitation of the body we cannot be greatly stirred by emotion. Others might say that the excitement of ideational centers would suffice. Unquestionably, the more vehement the passion, the more intense the cerebral excitement; and any great excitement in the brain can hardly fail to modify the whole attitude and expression of the man. It would be hard indeed, in such a case, to prove how much of the total consciousness is due to the rush of images in the fancy, and how much to the sense of strain in the body. The two factors commonly come together, and it would be necessary to isolate them to discover what is contributed by each. The hypothesis that all the emotional element comes from below the brain, and that the internal excitement of that organ would produce merely cold and intellectual perception, has certainly the charm of clearness and the merit of originality. It is so simple and luminous that one cannot help wishing it may be true. At the same time, what shall assure us that it does not abstract too much, or that the most limpid of the images of our fancy could ever have the tincture of emotion quite washed out of it?

These doctrines are perhaps the most distinctive and radical advanced by Professor James—those that make his book a real contribution to psychology, and undoubtedly the most important that has yet been made in America. But to mention them alone would convey a false impression of the tone and temper of the author, and of his general attitude in philosophy. His treatment of every subject is not equally radical and incisive; where his sympathies are engaged the edge of his criticism is blunted. One has but to turn from the discussion of space perception, for instance, to that of free will, automatism, or the nature of the soul, to mark the change. In regard to these matters Professor James is cautious, puzzled, and apologetic; and in making his final decision he is avowedly guided by his æsthetic and moral bias. Such procedure is not unphilosophic for one who believes, with Lotze, that our moral and emotional instincts are the best guides to ultimate truth. Of course the sceptic will smile at such convictions and murmur something about mysticism and superstition; and to hold such a faith and build upon it does, possibly, mar the unity and weaken the force of a treatise like this, the method of which is generally objective and experimental. But it would be pedantry to regret the loss of logical unity in a book so rich and living, in which a generous nature breaks out at every point, and the perennial problems of the human mind are discussed so modestly, so solidly, with such a deep and pathetic sincerity.

Many, no doubt, will begin these two thick volumes with a shudder at the labor in store; but those who persevere will read them with increasing interest and pleasure, and no one who can draw from them the instruction and inspiration they contain will close them without gratitude.

CROCE'S AESTHETICS

"Perhaps," says our author, upon finishing the theoretic part of his book,[1] or his theory of imagination, "perhaps the present treatment of aesthetics may seem rather meager when compared externally with the thick volumes that have usually been devoted to this science. But it is to be observed that, for nine-tenths of their bulk, those volumes are filled with irrelevant matter, such as psychological or metaphysical definitions of pseudo-aesthetic ideas (the sublime, the comic, the tragic, the humorous, etc.), or with expositions of an imaginary aesthetic zoology, botany and mineralogy, or with universal history appreciated aesthetically, and finally that the whole history of art and literature is dragged in (and in most cases distorted), together with critical remarks on Homer and Dante, on Ariosto and Shakespeare, on Beethoven and Rossini, on Michelangelo and Raphael—then our account, far from seeming too meager, will appear much ampler than those ordinary discussions which, after all, ignore or scarcely touch upon the greater number of difficult problems, properly aes-

[1] Benedetto Croce, *Estetica come scienza dell' espressione e linguistica generale*.

108

thetic, on which we have felt bound to spend our energies." [2]

The author's theory of aesthetic perception is in fact so
simple and radical that it might well have been explained
in one-tenth of those one hundred and fifty pages which
he devotes to it, and which are filled for the most part,
not, indeed, with appreciation of works of art, but with
criticism of other aesthetic theories. This criticism no
doubt helps to illustrate the contrasted cardinal tenet that
nothing is aesthetic except the art of intuition or imagination and that nothing is a work of art except the inner
momentary product of fancy. Yet this polemic, while it
bears witness to the author's firm grasp on the transcendental conditions of aesthetic experience, only serves to
make manifest the barrenness of any strictly transcendental
philosophy; for by insistence on the formal truism that
all art or beauty, to be actually appreciated, must fall
within a "transcendental unity of apperception," and by
reducing all aesthetic theory to this truism, most of the
problems with which critics deal are indeed banished from
"aesthetics" without, it must be confessed, being thereby
solved or particularly clarified.

Similar criticism is continued in the historical part of
the work which fills the remaining three hundred and
fifty pages. This survey is remarkably comprehensive, a
great number of writers and theories being noticed, especially those of recent times; but the history has a strongly
critical cast and serves chiefly to mark the relation between
the various schools and the author's own views. For this

[2] Page 143.

reason, probably, he despatches the Greeks in twenty pages, since, while he greatly admires Aristotle's proposal to distinguish the nature of art from that of science and history, he takes no interest in the problem which chiefly preoccupied ancient philosophers, namely, the place of art not in a psychological division of faculties, but in the ideal organization of life. The most novel and interesting point in this history is the prominence given to Vico and Schleiermacher. Vico, we learn, was the true founder of aesthetic science. For Vico had said: "Gli uomini prima *sentono* senz' avvertire; da poi *avvertiscono* con animo perturbato e commosso; finalmente *riflettono* con mente pura." This is Signor Croce's own fundamental philosophy, save that he does not show the same bias in favor of intellect. Schleiermacher, on the other hand, had said: "Das innere Bild ist das eigentliche Kunstwerk." This is another essential part of our author's doctrine.

Human life, we are told, moves on three distinct levels. The first is that of sensation or animal consciousness (not clearly distinguished by Signor Croce from unconscious or merely physiological processes) in which flux is absolute and nothing can be retained or discriminated from other things. The second level is that of apperception or intuition, in which attention and synthetic imagination have done their work and generated definite ideas. These ideas our author calls *expressions*, since they represent or render back some of the apparently unperceived impressions in the sentient stream. The third level is that of thought, the creation of concepts or universals. Thought has intuition for its basis, and all science, since science deals exclusively with universals, draws its materials from art. Art, on the other hand, is anterior to thought and independent of it, such concepts as enter, for instance, into a poem, being first melted down and reduced again to intuition before they can form part of a new imaginative creation.

Of these three levels, the first is sensuous and passionate (pleasure and pain belong there) and the third intellectual. The second alone is aesthetic, and consists entirely in intuition or expression. Such intuition or expression is art, always art, and the whole of art. Expression is painted on a background of feeling and is a product of mind or spirit; it does not belong to the natural world, like the impressions it interprets, but is lifted by the act of intuition into a higher plane, or rather projected into another dimension, which is that of aesthetic reality or art. Those material objects, like statues and pictures, which are ordinarily called works of art, are only external contrivances to stimulate aesthetic creation in the beholder and are no more works of art than the printed marks on a page are a poem. They serve merely to stimulate aesthetic performance by suggesting again the operation performed in a moment of vision by the creative artist and now to be perhaps reproduced in other moments of other lives when these are capable of appreciating and appropriating the heritage. But the true work of art is the act of expression itself, the living image evoked by the spirit. Art has no existence apart from active imagination.

Now this identification of art with aesthetic activity and of aesthetic activity with intuition or apperception of every sort has some interesting consequences. All men, we learn, are artists, and every attentive observation of a phenomenon is a work of art. Speech is art; linguistics and aesthetics are identical. We may be artists in our dreams but never in our labors. Technique, subject, associations, purposes, moral affinities are all irrelevant to the spiritual and poetic essence of beauty, which consists wholly in the momentary mastery which imagination gains over subconscious experience, through the synthesis of apprehension.

A further consequence is that when expression is successful beauty is perfect, no matter what the feeling is that is expressed. If the word "monkey" succeeds in rendering its underlying impressions as adequately as the word "star," the two intuitions and the two expressions are equally beautiful. We can see from this that our author's aesthetic theory is indeed a short and simple affair, and obviates a great deal of troublesome lucubration in philosophy and criticism. For it naturally follows that beauty has no relation to charm, to the attractive, or to the good. The charming or pleasant lies in the animal level or consciousness (or unconsciousness), while the good, we may suppose, belongs to the region of concepts. The expression of pain and evil, if it be adequate, is as beautiful as the expression of pleasure and the good, the pure aesthetic delight of perception may be superimposed equally on every sort of sensuous and moral value. The author does not deny that sensuous and rational considerations may have legitimate weight in determining our attitude towards those products of manufacture vulgarly called works of art; we may, on such non-aesthetic grounds, justly refuse to look at an object at all; but its beauty will nevertheless subsist, unqualified by those adventitious feelings. A thing painful to sense and morally repulsive may yet be entirely beautiful.

In view of such conclusions the reader cannot suppress the suspicion that the system before him is artificial. It emphasizes, to be sure, the active function of perception in a way which will appeal to sincere and introspective natures. Imaginative experience, in its abstract immediacy, is obviously present throughout to the author's mind. The pleasures inherent in that perceptive activity are those most characteristically aesthetic, and it is intelligible that a transcendentalist, neglecting the ulterior functions of things, should wish to limit the value of art to that formal and subjective element. But the point of real importance is not to reiterate some transcendental futility about the necessity, in any case, of imaginative action; the point, in all discriminating criticism, is rather to discover what materials, what scope, and what ulterior fruits imaginative action has in a given instance. The pleasures of sense, the charm and the functions of objects, even if denied an aesthetic status, will endure in the mind that judges and feels, unless, indeed, that mind has been reduced to a state of affected aestheticism and unintelligence. Ulterior judgment, practical and moral, will inevitably color every perception given to a rational creature. To say that such simultaneous human reactions do not affect *aesthetic* feeling is to walk the tight rope of artificial distinctions. A tripartite division of the soul, laid down by the psychologist, will not prevent all the elements present in experience from affecting the beauty, charm and perfection of the objects about which imagination may play, or from rendering them now wholly gracious and beautiful, now utterly trivial and vile. Nor is that tripartite division of the soul, even technically considered, anything but a convenient artifice. Man does not feel without distinguishing nor distinguish and see without thinking and knowing. Life is sure, in these matters, to take its revenge upon scholasticism, and the more punctiliously a department has been cut off from the general society of the mind, the more will that department be reduced to insignificance. If intuition has nothing to do with sense or with reason, so much the worse for intuition. An art which is nothing but an irresponsible and private exercise of fancy on every occasion becomes a visionary indulgence, a trick not of genius, but of incapacity halting in the middle of life.

This situation is well illustrated in what Signor Croce has to tell us about language. A word, he says, being an expression, a synthesis reached by creative genius, is not a sign. But he would admit, I suppose, that it may ultimately become a sign; and its destiny in that respect is precisely what renders language steadily and usefully articulate and different from music. If speech never became symbolic it would remain in that region of irrecoverable scintillations and dreams which is still haunted by the music and vague suggestions of poetry; it would not have become an instrument for practical communication and rational discourse. Though prose be but an afterthought, prose fortunately exists, and we cannot very well deny that to communicate ideas is a function which even "aesthetic" language occasionally subserves. Discourse without concepts and objects without charm may be momentarily sufficient for that contemptible entity, the abstract poet, whose mind is a barren kaleidoscope for the endless intuition of everything, but they are nevertheless singularly tedious to the sensitive, political, and thinking animal properly called man.

ON METAPHYSICAL
PROJECTION

by which Existence is referred to

the Non-Existent as to its Ground

THE ABOVE TITLE gives a brief exposition of a large subject: how much it involves may be suggested by a few critical comparisons.

I. THE ONTOLOGICAL HIERARCHY

At the bottom is matter, the seat and
organ of all manifestations.

Ontologically the place and character which I assign to existence are the same assigned to it, if I may trust reports, by the orthodox doctrines of India. Pure Being, or Brahma, since it is eternal and undivided, is an essence, not a substance or existence. This essence has infinite potential manifestations, each a different essence containing pure Being, and all together forming the realm of essence. Of these potential manifestations some may remain unmanifested, and others may obtain a manifestation still of an unsubstantial sort. The grossest manifestation of Being is the material world, of which man's animal nature is a part. This material world not only exists and changes but by so doing becomes the occasion and root of all the manifestations of Being, in their partiality, contingence, and alternation. But the material world exists and changes blindly, since the essences embodied in it continually mix and vary without being ever discerned.

Next is appearance, or essences manifested to sense and to thought.

A subtler manifestation of Being lies in appearance, when certain essences become specious presences and are actively distinguished, but by an intuition which is a function of animal life, so that the essences appearing are probably not conceived in their purity and eternity but are identified with the outlying material things on which the animal's action or instinct is for the moment directed. This hasty identification is normal, since discourse has no terms in which to designate things except these specious essences; but the same illusion, with the trepidation involved, persists idly in dreams, where there is no relevant material object, and no occasion for action or belief. Appearances are accordingly not always quite satisfactory signs for their material occasions or objects, and are sometimes, from a practical point of view, called unreal or illusory: but ontologically specious objects, being essences, are on a higher plane than material objects or than other existing facts; and a free mind, viewing appearances squarely, would find no hint of existence in them. It is the intuition of them, or the fact of their appearing, that exists and lapses, remaining attached to matter by its occasion and root in the dreamer's body.

Next is truth, or the aspect which the
universe would wear to omniscience.

Immediately above appearance there is a still subtler embodiment of Being, not particular and occasional, like the perceptions and dreams of animals, yet in a different way still dependent on material existence: this is the realm of truth. It includes so much of Being or essence as an omniscient intellect would perceive to be manifested in all the worlds ever existing, including all the categories and relations implicit in them. This manifestation, itself non-existent, impersonal and eternal, is the highest of which Being is capable: beyond it we should come to unmanifested Being.

Next is the realm of essence, including
all unmanifested Being.

This is the realm of essence: when we reach it we are again in the open, contingency and fact having dropped out of view: for here all unmanifested modes of Being are on the same footing exactly as those which happen to be manifested; although from a worldly and unspeculative point of view essences never manifested are of no interest; as indeed most of those manifested are also, when not useful as signs for probable events on the human scale.

Finally, at the top, is pure Being itself.

Yet this is not the end of the story. Even within the realm of essence there is a hierarchy, in which pure Being appears at the summit. It is like the extension in which all geometrical figures are contained undistinguished, or the marble block in which all statues are sleeping. This sort of inclusion seems empty to a desultory mind that needs to perceive things separately in order to perceive them at all, because it is trained to watch only for existences, and existence requires exclusion. But the dialectician, in studying any essence, sees various complementary features, no less concrete than those included in it, which this essence expressly excludes; and just as he feels how much richer the realm of essence is, though unmanifested, than the one essence with which his contemplation began; so the sage capable of intense concentration finds in any element of any essence, that is, in pure Being, room and depth enough for all the distinctions which are not, but might be, actualized within it. As youth, in its universal readiness, is freer and juster than maturity, and infinitely more beautiful, so pure Being, in its indistinction, is more complete than any more special essence, which in choosing one determination excludes all the others. Even among essences, individuality is profoundly arbitrary, almost scandalous; and in the simplicity of pure Being there is a sublime recollection and impartiality, as if it denied each only because it remembered all.

This hierarchy marks the steps of a spiritual progress.

As these last phrases suggest, the interest of this ontology is not merely logical, in that it defines the order of a possible world, as we might frame rules for a new game. It represents faithfully the stages of an actual spiritual

progress: I will not say the only path of progress open
to the human soul, because life is elastic; but certainly the
path hitherto most familiar and sacred. Life carries every
sensitive animal as far up as appearance; intelligence raises
him, at least in intention, to the level of truth; contemplation lifts him to that of essence, and ecstasy into the heart
of pure Being. But this ascent is internal to experience, it
is a transformation of allegiances, of spiritual possessions
and worship. It is not a material translation from one part
of the universe to another, where a new set of material
objects assaults us and forces us to become selfless and
pure. If the beggar had actually become king, he would
need to begin then at the bottom of his spiritual progress,
until he was perfectly content to become a beggar again:
sitting in his rags it will be as easy or easier for him to be
translated into heaven; his bliss must be renunciation, his
kingship insight.

*Double use of "manifestation": substance is
manifested by its formations and effects,
essence is manifested in its instances.*

I have used the word "manifestation": this might mean
that some sign betrayed an underlying state of substance,
as putrefaction is manifested by a bad smell; or it might
mean that, by chance or through unknown causes, some
essence is exemplified in appearance, as beauty is exemplified in light. Now rot is a cause of smells, but beauty is
not a cause of light but *vice versa;* and in general we may
say that when the manifestation is of a substance it is an
effect of the thing manifested; but when an essence is

manifested that essence is an immaterial being altogether remote from the level of flux and causation, the cause of its manifestation being, as in the other case, some state of substance beneath. Thus in every instance manifestation is double-faced, like Janus: the smell, too, exemplifies an essence which does not cause it, namely, this precise quality of pungency and evil, with all the simpler essences contained in it, up to pure Being (which evil manifests as much as good does, and which therefore transcends them); and on the other hand, the light which exemplifies beauty is not without its natural causes, in the sun and the ether; and its very sublimation into beauty, when this occurs, has its causes in the human eye and heart, naturally happy to see the light, and to see by it.

*No essence can be the antecedent cause
or ground of its manifestations.*

There would therefore be a vast confusion and subversion of all understanding if we identified the ontological hierarchy culminating in pure Being, a hierarchy of essences manifested inwardly to the spirit, with the natural causes of our existence, or spiritual capacity, so that our spirit comes one day to be favored with that manifestation. Pure Being, the realm of essence, and the truth are in themselves non-existent and unmanifested; and even in appearance, if there is something existent, it is not the specious being manifested, but the active intuition or feeling of some animal, led by his organic life and surroundings to conceive—that is, to dream—those appearances: for dreams would be impossible if all consciousness, in its

proper nature, were not a dream. To mistake the ontological hierarchy for a dynamic set of antecedents, which
bring about all the manifestations of Being, would be to
repeat the illusion by which given essences are supposed
to be the things that produce the intuition of those essences. Cause, in metaphysics, has many meanings: and it
would be quite true to say that pure Being, and all its
ontological specifications, were the formal or the final
cause of their appearance; since in them their appearance
finds its full expression and quietus: but confusion begins
when these ideal vanishing-points are substituted for the
efficient and material cause of the appearance, which in its
last sublimation may end in them.

All powers are substances and parts of nature.

If pure Being had ever been first in time, as it is first in
logic, nothing else could have come to be, not even time.
Positivistic religions, like the Jewish, may think of God
as a creator and governor of the world, because theirs is
a living God, a part of nature, ontologically perfectly contingent and material, and revealed by his acts, such as
thunder and legislation and miracles: and he may be ap-
proached and conversed with on occasion, or seen on his
throne in the heavenly Jerusalem. But the dialectic of the
spiritual life, while not in the least incompatible with that
monarchical theism, has a first or ultimate object of quite
another kind. This subsists in the minds of Jewish and
Christian mystics side by side with their positivistic faith;
and in the Indians tends to predominate. They tell us, for
instance, that in deep sleep a man may be identified with

Brahma, but only passively because (having still a body) he can awake and revert to his habitual imaginations: had he become identical with Brahma in fact, or by a positive insight, like the sage who has annulled all his illusions by viewing them together and seeing them to be all illusions, he could never again believe; he could never again descend to distinct imagination or divided existence. In a word, *there is no way down from heaven to earth, from Being to existence.* Existence can exist, and can be posited, only from the point of view of the part. The eternal is not just outside our home park, beyond the eastern and the western gate: beyond, on that level, there are only other stretches and more weariness, or else nothing. The eternal hangs above and opens everywhere within; it comes not by observation, but by self-knowledge and self-denial.

So much for the projection of an ontological hierarchy, marking stages of spiritual emancipation, into a metaphysical world beyond the natural world, or taking its place. The fable is transparent. The supremacy of eternal things is moral and logical, not causal; and it would be impossible to pass genetically from pure Being and its modes (even if hypostatized into eternal substances) to things contingent, changeful, and existent.

II. TRANSCENDENTALISM

In transcendentalism the casual forms of intuition, grammar, or history are projected into the a priori.

In another way, much more curious and unexpected, existence is derived in the transcendental philosophy from the non-existent. Since this philosophy is psychological, existence in its view is confined to experience; and the nerve of its transcendentalism lies in finding *a priori* principles to which experience is compelled to conform, and which make it possible for it to arise. Chief among these principles are space and time which, according to Kant, are the *a priori* forms of intuition; that is to say, every object of intuition must exhibit a specious extension or duration or both; and, besides, it must occupy some particular portion of a single space and a single time, within which, by an *a priori* decree of reason, everything admitted to exist must find its place. Much that I have said above may seem to repeat these doctrines. Have I not spoken of a cosmic system outside of which nothing can belong to the sphere of action? And have I not shown at length that specious space and time are animal perspectives,[1] that is to say, forms imposed on things by the need of synthesizing them from one point of view, and not proper to things in their true dispersion? Yes: but there are differences. Kant was not an impressionist: he did not notice the actual essences given in sense and fancy, with their vague multiplicity of placeless extensions and dateless times: his conventional intellect beheld nothing but one solid seamless continuum, in its Newtonian infinity and rigor. His *a priori* forms and categories were worse than his categorical imperative; for if the latter imposed universal duties, it left people magnificently free to disre-

---

[1] See *The Realm of Matter*, Chapter IV, "Pictorial Space and Sentimental Time." [D.C.]

gard them: whereas the *a priori* rules of intuition were coercive, apparently, everywhere and for ever over all dreamers, angels, animals, and poets. Why this uniformity in fancy, which is the freest of things? Nature and habit may be monotonous, and their forms, once acquired, may change but slowly; and perhaps an appearance may be said to be determined *a priori* when its form can be foretold, and turns up as expected. But animal senses, if they vary slowly, are very various: lives, dreams, ideas are broken and, in their instant burden, are incommunicable: why should they not be of all sorts? The only control which I can conceive exercised over intuition is that exercised by matter. If we suppose that types of imagination go with types of character and behavior, imagination might be compelled, under pain of extinction, not to change too fast or stray too far so long as nature was constant, and to adapt itself as ingeniously and good-humoredly as possible to the new environment, when nature had changed. But I am reverting to common sense: let me continue the argument.

Fatal consequence that the flux of nature is specious, and that intuition cannot be repeated in separate instances.

Intuition is a poetic act, life budding into images: its objects are momentary, evanescent, unsubstantial, unless indeed we fly with them to their home sky, where they are eternal. What then could seem more perverse than to maintain that the forms of intuition are fixed *a priori*, and must all yield portions of one stark mathematical ghost, geometrical space and time? Yet worse is to come: for if this specious space and time are the space and time of nature, nature too must be specious: a synthesis of appearances made in intuition. Then the diremption of Being into existence—the division, transition, generation, conflict, and lapse which are its very pulses—can belong only to appearance; and the actual moments of experience cannot be deployed in any medium, cannot be many, successive, or collateral, since there is no multiplicity or relation possible save in the specious medium which intuition imposes on its imagined terms, in their specious synthesis. What? Has intuition no instances? In this philosophy of experience are there no real events? Are the *a priori* forms of logic not employed more than once in thinking? If they are, how are the thoughts themselves related? Certainly not within the landscape which they paint, framing it in the transcendental unity of their intuition. The thoughts arise, of course, swim and sink, in the flux of existence: the whole transcendental philosophy describes, and can describe, only the perspectives open to each of those thoughts, according to the force and method of fancy within them: but as to the seat, origin, existence and variety of these thoughts it must be silent, or can utter only confusion.

Transcendental logic is a logic internal to perspectives.

The philosopher may raise a monument as vast as he will; it will be his prison while he lives, and his tomb afterwards. He may paint its walls with a panorama of the universe, but he cannot include himself painting it—

except perhaps in a playful episode in one corner: and then that miniature will not be at all the inclusive enacted event, the actual episode in the life of nature, which contained himself, his monument, his model, and his painting. History synthesized in the historian's mind is but a single incident in the march of history: yet both the flux of events and the inspirations of Clio are called "history" on occasion; and to this equivocation transcendental philosophy, which loves to be historical, owes all its specious profundity. The logical unities of intuition and theory are substituted everywhere for the chaotic current of events. The external relations, transitive and multifarious, proper to flux and to existence, are hidden under the mask of some dramatic essence, superstitiously regarded as the secret of those facts—an essence in which of course the parts are mutually responsive and essential to the whole. Thus once more the non-existent is projected metaphysically to be the ground of existence.

Nature subsists outside, and its substance is not pure Being, but matter posited in action.

Sometimes when this equivocation is avoided (as it was by Kant himself) another takes its place. If all forms of sense and thought are subjective, the inference may be drawn that substance, since it cannot be in specious space or time, must be some Absolute thing, single and indivisible. This inference is erroneous. Pure Being is indeed single and indivisible, because it is the essence having those essential characters given in intuition; for that reason it is not a substance. Substance is something posited in action and problematical in its inner nature. To assert that it must be one or devoid of relations is to contradict the only reason there is for positing it. The inference also shows a backsliding into the habit of hypostatizing given essences: the very habit which critical and psychological philosophy came to correct. A momentary blank may be left in intuition, if I attempt to banish from it all spatial and temporal images; but even if this blank were permanent and irreparable (which it is not) it would only prove the poverty of my imagination by which only *these* spatial and temporal images could be framed: it would not condemn substance to have no parts or properties. To assign to it the non-entity which may confront me when I dismiss my most familiar fancies is as if a child, on hearing that perhaps God does not think in English, should be driven to the shocking conclusion that God must think in French. Substance, let me repeat, is not an object of intuition, but of animal faith, and the alternatives of intuition do not dominate it. What we know of it is that it fulfills a certain function in the world of action and in our inner life, precisely the function of distributing and diversifying the events in these fields, so that the existence of each part is intrinsic yet conditioned by the existence and character of its neighbors. Specious space and time can, for that reason, serve to express imaginatively the true constitution of nature: they transcribe graphically the genetic distribution of things and their coexistences. Animals and their intuitions grow up in the retinue of these material events and are indices to them. If fancy dresses up nature in some respects, it simplifies nature enormously in others. How could we give different names to things if things in themselves had no distinctions? How could they affect us variously if they were all identical? Specious space and time, like other essences given in intuition, have a literary function in the universe; most excellent when most original and selective, but also when most significant; for the beauty of discourse is to abbreviate the facts verbally and to enlarge them humorously. But how should literature abolish the world which it comes to describe, or reduce to a blank or a block all that is not poetry?

III. THE THEORY OF RELATIVITY

All appearances and measures are, as in the theory of relativity, relative to the observer.

Something of transcendentalism seems to be lurking in the theory of relativity; the haste and zeal with which it has been acclaimed in some quarters makes one suspicious. At many points my contentions, based on quite different grounds, seem to coincide with this theory: that existence has many centers, that specious space and time (in their Newtonian form or in any other) cannot be expected to mirror absolutely the true structure of nature; that the flux of substance combines change and collateral relations more intimately than do the space and time of our imagination, which are quite separable in thought; that transit along a path, as in radiation, is an autonomous process, measurable by internal changes, which supply the scale of the movement and the rhythmic intervals determined by "clocks"; and that to these material measures and intervals our habit of intuition must adapt itself, if it is to be closely applicable to the description of facts: all these aspects of relativity seem congruous with the doctrine that human experience and science are spiritual responses in an animal to a material world quite beyond their jurisdiction, but controlling their development. So taken, relativity merely means that appearances are relative to the centers from which they appear, and that measurements are relative to the rods and clocks used in making them, the centers being dynamically related in a single cosmos, surveyed from different points of vantage within it. If each map of the world is relative to the system of projection on which it is drawn, relativity would seem to imply a common original, which each rendering transforms according to its special perspective. These distortions may be normal and regular, and in no way misleading or incompatible: their diversity may be a consequence of their accuracy, seeing that each applies a special measure from a special point of origin to their common field. Relativity will prevail in the realm of perspectives and opinions, where nothing else could possibly prevail: but things will not be absorbed by those views, for the very reason that the views are relative.

In so far as they convey knowledge, all views refer to a common world, which is that in which action goes on.

But perhaps these are platitudes unworthy of a revolutionary age. Does not relativity rather mean that every center of observation or reference is absolved from co-ordination with any other, since nothing can appear to it save its own terms? In this case the name of relativity should have been absolutism, since each center would be the center of a different universe, determined beyond the possibility of comparison or control by the essences figuring in that perspective; it would not be the description of an existence beyond itself, of which other perspectives might be descriptions also. Natural science, like mathematics, would be a study of essence, without any ulterior object. No doubt the systems, or rather their authors, might be subject to pragmatic tests in the human world; and by a sort of social courtesy or animal timidity they might recognize one another's existence, and by a supra-scientific communion of saints they might drink in, or spew out, one another's systems: but these mundane contacts would need to be quickly transliterated into the terms of science, that is, into the perspective view of them that could be integrated into each center.

Or is the theory of relativity an optical metaphysics, with transcendental functions attributed to light?

The dominant position assigned to light seems to support this interpretation of relativity. If the velocity of light is assumed to be invariable and the absolute maximum of velocity possible in nature, it would seem to be because, in astronomy, light-signals are the only witnesses to facts: facts not so transmissible cannot be reported at all, and therefore are excluded from science. But how should they be excluded from nature by any such transcendental condition, unless transcendentalism has already identified nature with the constructions of the naturalist, and denied that any nature exists in which these constructions themselves are incidents? Yet even from a transcendental point of view the supremacy assigned to light seems excessive: if it is the sole medium of communication with the heavens, the case is not the same on earth or in animal life. There is a groping science that begins at home, and finds its proofs there; and this is the only science that has existent things for its object. It would be a curious complication indeed if domestic matters like chewing and digestion, before they could become objects of knowledge, required to be expressed astronomically in terms of pure optics, and to be measured, though they occur in the dark, by the velocity of light. After all it is on earth, not in the heavens, that we exist and are in the thick of existence; it is only by supposing a material influence, not the actual optical image, passing from the stars to us that we recognise the stars to be substances, that is, objects not merely specious but materially conditioning their own appearance. Light itself is such a material agency, not the seen splendor of light. But perhaps what is still called science may be a metaphysics resting on a sensualistic logic, and built up by a mathematical calculus; a system bound to be pictorial at all costs, and like psychological idealism conceiving bodies to be composed of those visual images which signal their presence to us from a distance. Such is the homage which, in the last stages of intellectual anarchy, algebraic ingenuity can pay to an affectation of innocence or to a literary impressionism. But impressions themselves are not ultimate existences: they are ultimate only when their deliverance is reduced to a pure essence, conveying no fact. Taken as reports of existences, or as existing objects, all impressions are poetical in spite of the impressionist. Only a visionary world can be composed out of them; its elements, as well as its laws, will be essences hypostatized, some of them given, but most of them begged and interpolated *ad libitum* according to the requirements of the theory. Each of these constructions will be a possible world exhumed from the realm of essence; each scientific philosopher will pursue his private speculations, with his esoteric system of notation, perhaps unintelligible to every other philosopher; unless indeed a scientific Soviet should be led by some subtle political instinct to adopt a particular mathematical dream and impose it on the lay world. Animal instinct will never cease to use all fine images and languages as signs for the material things which fill the field of action. "Science" too, in so far as it is a calculus applicable to crude facts, may figure among those picturesque popular beliefs which I call knowledge of existence, not because they are not symbolic in texture and essentially fantastic, but because being so they are truly symbolic in intent and in function. The rest of each "scientific" system, like a new theology, will be a maze of essences projected by the technical imagination and deputed to be the ground of material things.

*Practical, symbolic, and literary status
of all natural knowledge.*

That the impassioned users of symbols are often deceived by them, and become idolaters, is an ancient experience. It is an indignity to the soul; yet little practical
harm will ensue so long as the wise habits accompanying
that illusion are not deranged by it. In this way religions
have proved friendly to human life; in this way Euclid
has long endeared himself to builders and navigators; and
so the most extravagant imaginations of "science" may
do in their day. Common sense, if questioned about its
beliefs, will reply idolatrously, but if not questioned will
take those beliefs quite symbolically: so "science," while
scholastically projecting the terms which appear in its
theories into a world above the world of action, may
serve in the arts to expedite action and to give it intellectual expression. The title of relativity might then remind
the metaphysician that he was a member of a nondescript
human herd, and that his system was relative to himself,
an odd transcription of the world in which men live together; so that Heraclitus would have said that in his
philosophizing he was dreaming and only in his arts was
awake. I would not be disrespectful of dreams. When,
like the Vision of Dante, dreams synthesize experience
rather than interrupt it, they may be better than pedestrian
observation. So perhaps the movements and cross-lights of
nature, calculated from any one arbitrary point, may make
a more marvelous kaleidoscopic system than vulgar materialism; and in so far as these mathematical exercises

limber up the mind, startle our moral sloth, and accustom us to conceive nature in strange ways, remote from the human scale, I think they can be nothing but salutary. They convince us of our relativity: they vivify this conventional world in which we move about so nimbly but so blindly; they fill it with the tremor of a friendly mystery, as if primeval Spring were astir in it, and the immortal Gods.

HUMAN SYMBOLS
FOR MATTER

THOSE WISE MEN who knew the language of birds might have conferred a boon upon philosophy: they might have taught us how very different are the ways in which the same thing may be said. Perhaps a musician intervening might pronounce it foolish to talk of *understanding* the birds, as if they sang program-music: a sympathetic stranger should merely listen, and retain some subtle cadence or some wild note for his own repertory. If this musician became a philosopher, he might extend the same principle to his own utterance, and to the whole experience of mankind, graphic or emotional. All would form an aesthetic foreground, signifying nothing. Human bird-notes, called perceptions and thoughts, would compose the human universe, and the mere suggestion of anything beyond would be nonsense. To the pure poet the world is indeed a great spectacle, loaded inexplicably with laughter and tears: and there is a spectacular physics and a literary metaphysics which, if consistent, would also stop at that. These superior minds can afford to mean nothing. So richly to exist is enough.

But meantime the artisan, the sailor, the husbandman know nature by co-operation, for which inspection gives only a signal: to them matter has dimensions which are not merely picturesque: it works in secret, and is full of omens and potentialities. Although practice sharpens the eye, and multiplies the features in an object which are felt to be significant, yet their significance swallows up their observable form: and it is only in some rare moment, and with shame, that the weather-eye can become poetical, or the reading-eye stop to notice the print. Perhaps the birds are in this case, and the pure musician may not have understood their anxieties; he may be more bird-witted than they. Their speech may not be merely vocal: perhaps by their music they warn one another or address the gods in whom they believe. Perhaps they even anticipate the gods' answers; some oracle borne through the air may have a dim sense for them, to be clarified afterwards by events: for the words proper to a god are the strokes of fortune. A friend of birds would need to understand all this in the birds' way; and then, by a sudden luminous analogy, he might come to understand, as if from a distance, the too familiar language of man.

In a modern literary mind, things and persons are dissolved into subtler elements, and the prevalent symbols for matter are of two disparate kinds: there are optical pictures of things, confused in current philosophy with their substance; and there are imputed psychological processes, also regarded as substantial, and as going on by themselves. These two sets of symbols are indeed convenient and inevitable in the present phase of human intelligence: but a philosopher need not make idols of them, nor prefer them to the richer and more beautiful idols familiar to his ancestors. Of the material objects confronting us in action, and of our own bodies, we *cannot* have ideas at all adequate or literal: if we kept to the ideas of science, we should live in a whirligig of squeaking manikins. In order to understand what happens and what we do, we need a moral mythology: and the ancients needed one also in order to understand the great movements of nature, which they could hardly conceive to be mechanical. A great development of language, religion, poetry, and ceremony enabled early man to render his mind articulate: and to him we owe the humanities, and humanity itself.

How living, how appropriate, how complete for human purposes such rhetoric could be, we may see in those regions where we still employ it, as we do in human society. Suppose I am boxing with a friend; my perceptions of his motions and my vague but subtle sense of his temperament and disposition suffice for my action. I have no sense of being in the presence of an obscure and profound object. A sporting man, I say to myself, is only too easily known: he is like a school primer, very simple, very one-sided, and issued by the thousand. Yet how enormously inadequate are all my literary notions to the movements that must be actually going on in him and in me, and to the intertwining instincts of battle and sport, latent and inbred in such a contest! I am not boxing—though an idealist should say so—with my idea of my friend. My fugitive notions of him are entirely composed of his looks, words, and traits of character: yet none of these essences could possibly give or receive a blow. Their relevance to action depends on their relevance to matter. The man's character counts only as, for the moment, it means quickness or hesitation in his sparring, predictability or looseness in his attitude. All that I have seen or heard of him counts only in so far as it supports my tacit assumptions regarding his competence and fairness. Far beneath all this mental rumor, our instinctive conduct hangs on intricate affinities and reactions in us, existing directly on the plane of matter; only they cannot be expressed in human discourse otherwise than by naming some conventional moral quality or general habit. By the application of names, and the intrusion of curt judgments, the picture of existence comes together in our minds. Our perceptions are like those great stitches in coarse white thread with which tailors baste the lining of our garments; they do for trying on; they prefigure the result; but beneath them and beside them there must be continuity in the stuff, and tight material stitching of quite another color, matching the texture of the stuff itself, and indistinguishable from it.

Human symbolism is original, poetical, arbitrary, but at the same time it is inevitably significant and expressive of material fact; and it has these two characters not alternately, so that the more musical it is the less it signifies, but concurrently; so that, as we see in the case of mathematics, its free logical development, when the primary theme is well chosen, may serve to traverse the whole complexity of nature with a remarkable fidelity, though of course only in some special transcript, leaving the substance of nature out. This correspondence of genius with truth is no miracle of pre-established harmony. Genius is precisely this union of great spontaneity and inner power, with great sensitiveness and sympathy for the nature of things outside: a union which is possible and normal, because the psyche is a part of the material world, an anagram of it, and expands, in so far as she may, in harmony with her conditions. Her song, her language, her feelings are therefore likely to become more expressive, and fitter to serve as terms in knowledge, in proportion as they grow more limpid, and mark more clearly her own rhythms and spontaneous growth. Here, perhaps, we may see some natural justification for that mystic assurance, often so hollow, that beauty is truth, truth beauty. They are entirely different: but a beautiful medium, being in harmony with human nature, is more likely than an ugly medium to be in harmony with nature at large.

Persons are things that can move and speak. For the physician or the statesman they need never be anything more: he can roughly calculate their conduct and perhaps modify it by appropriate treatment. Each of us in his own person, when passive or ill, accepts this conception of his nature: he asks to be treated like a thing; he wishes his reactions and feelings to be controlled for him, and restored to a normal harmony with the ambient influences. Of these he then feels himself to be a momentary conjunction, strident or luminous. He recognizes his antecedent impotence over himself, all his energy being their energies conjoined: and he looks to medicine, to discipline, to divine grace for the strength to live prosperously, or to live at all.

When health returns this religious pathos is obscured, like the stars by day: and the individual life forges on, conscious of being master over itself, and over a large part of the world. It is so in reality, when once it is initiated and set in motion. There is no substance more substantial than that which is at work in each organism, and no energy more free. All are members of one family, sowing and reaping, marrying and having children; and they can live on in a happy stupidity, as if moved by nothing deeper than their customs and the round of the seasons. It is only when they quarrel, or when disease or ruin overtakes them, that they begin to perceive that those rapid conventions were not on the scale of nature, even of nature in their own persons: and they rise or fall to another level of organization, and to thinking on another scale.

A person, or a group of persons, is a definite center of influence: another person feels that presence as a unit, and reacts and forms expectations towards that unit as a whole, without discriminations of elements or reasons. But this is a sort of scent, or *flair:* when language or reflection attempts to account for it, the person or group must be distinguished into certain passions, purposes, or imputable guiding thoughts, to which to attach the expected actions. Divination, policy, and intrigue often play with these conventional units not unsuccessfully: but policy is not an exact science, and it drops many a feather—all, at last— in its flight. Its flutterings compose the lamentable history of nations and of designing minds. Sensible people, whose reactions remain massive and who do not press their own thoughts, nor trust other people's, are obliged to use the same moral terms as the moralists or partisans: but they are saved from fanatical pedantries by a certain tacit translation of those moral terms into their material equivalents. Nations to them are simply peoples, philosophers men, passions fevers, religions institutions. Reducing all imaginative fictions to these mundane terms, they certainly miss the eloquence of those fictions and of the passions that created them; but that which they miss may be negligible in calculating the material issue; it may belong to the backwater or the shifting sands in the stream, or to its picturesque aspects, important only to the idle poet standing on the bank. Moral facts have a physical basis, not discernible in them intrinsically: they may therefore be translated into physical terms, no doubt also symbolical and summary, without losing the general thread of their sequence and of their consequences. To read moral facts in moral terms is perhaps the function of the novelist: but to read them in physical terms would be the function of the psychologist or biologist, if he were scientific: because it is only by virtue of their physical basis and relations that moral facts belong to the world at all, and take their place in history. Hence those historians who appreciate the kind of reality proper to dramatic events and to moral revolutions will never dissociate them from the material incidents and monuments which express and record them. Otherwise the historian would be an irresponsible poet and there would be no evidence that his story was true.

The consequences of attributing to others, and often to oneself, fictitious passions and sounding ideas are less serious than might be innocently supposed. Errors about immaterial facts can have no direct consequences whatsoever; and the consequences of the concomitant acts are mitigated by two circumstances. On the one hand, the absence of such ideas or passions *from the mind* does not imply that consonant dispositions may not exist unconsciously in the person or other region of nature to which they are attributed; in that case he who imputes the thought is symbolically more discerning than he who honestly denies it, in his ignorance of self. On the other hand, even the imputation of the wrong *unconscious* passion or idea may be useful in clarifying the attitude of the myth-maker himself; as superstitions about oaths or ties of blood may help to keep men steady, or belief in the devil to keep them wary, or as the illusion of being liked may keep them amiable. It is particularly in the organization of one's own purposes (as we see in politics) that myths about the passions and ideas of others play a useful part. Through the moral landscape thus fantastically painted a man may for the first time distinguish his own path, name his goal, and define his ideal enemies. He may say: *écraser l'infâme,* or *le cléricalisme, voilà l'ennemi:* phrases not descriptive of anything definite or real in the religious world, but excellent symbols for a particular lay policy. If a philosopher were interested in understanding the various phases of spirit, such subjective catchwords would be fatal but in action people are really interested only in transforming the material world of nature or of society, and their grossest misconceptions of spiritual facts are harmless for their purpose, if the material effect of uttering them is satisfactory.

Passions and ideas are conceived to animate persons and to render their conduct more nearly explicable. But the rest of nature also stands in need of such interpretation; the language of sense is far from adequate to trace the movements of matter; where it fails, and these movements are nevertheless important to human well-being, they have to be expressed in moral terms: and this necessity is the vulgar disproof of materialism. I say the vulgar disproof, although the subtlest philosophers employ it; because it is a vulgar prejudice to identify matter with the images of sense, when in reality sights and sounds are as fantastic transfigurations of matter in intuition as are words or religions. If touch does come nearer to the essence of matter, this is not due to its sensuous deliverance, which is almost nothing, but to its close association with action, and with the actual appropriation, as in eating, of the substance of one creature by another. It is precisely the incapacity of sense to trace these dark processes within and around that obliges us to sketch nature impressionistically, in large masses and conventional figures. Passions and ideas are then read into things, and yield the gods of mythology or the laws of nature. A law is an unconscious idea supposed to govern the movements of matter; and a god is a passion or purpose, now spasmodic, now pertinacious, running through a series of events, as they concern the worshiper. Laws and gods may be conceived impulsively, as powers; their existence and energy are then obvious, and directly posited by animal faith: they are matter under a popular rhetorical mask. But laws and gods may also be conceived critically, as forms exhibited by events, equations or harmonies which are not powers but descriptions of the results of power, if power be admitted into a critical philosophy at all. So conceived, laws and gods are immaterial; they are essences. They may be true of existence in some perspective or at some level; but the question of their existence on their own account never arises, being incongruous with their nature. They are simply forms proper to the realm of matter.

When a deity is conceived to be a spirit, like the God of Aristotle, its relation to matter becomes more subtle, like that of spirit to matter in ourselves: but the relation subsists, otherwise there would be no occasion for supposing that such a deity existed. The divine intellect, according to Aristotle, was wholly immaterial, changeless, and therefore materially inactive; but it realized in thought the form which the material world aspired to realize by its order and motion. It is in the measure in which this cosmic or hygienic harmony is realized in matter that the divine spirit is temporally and partially reproduced in us; and it might seem that this reproduction was the first and only actual realization of spirit, the so-called divine spirit, without an organ, eternal, and identical with its object, being only an essence. But Aristotle conceived that matter could not take a form unless that form had already pre-existed; and therefore the spirit could not appear imperfectly on earth unless it existed first in perfection beyond the heavens. This view is not now likely to find defenders, since it defies that sense of radical flux and indefinite variability which fills the modern soul; but even if we admitted it, we should have, in the existence of such a perfect divine intellect above the world, a remarkable witness to the character of the material world beneath it. For if this world were the magic effect of such a divine intellect, burning for ever clear and immutable, the order of this world would have to be, as Aristotle thought it, itself eternal; and disorder would be only an unmeaning oscillation or flurry due to a native incapacity in matter quite to sustain its prescribed forms. The most transcendent of gods, and the purest conceivable spirit, would thus be still a counterpart to the realm of matter and a sign of its secret harmonies.

The other forms assigned to deity by religion or philosophy are even more clearly personifications of material agencies, either in the world at large or in some special or ulterior part of it. When I speak of the realm of matter I must not be supposed to limit it to so much of nature as science may have recognized in the past or in the present or in the future. Science is expected to give evidence for its assertions: and why should the world throughout space and throughout past and future time be open to our inspection? By the realm of matter I understand the whole system of forces in which our action, to its remotest conditions or consequences, is embosomed: it therefore contains all so-called supernatural regions and powers, if they truly exist and could be reached by an exploration sufficiently subtle and prolonged. The heaven and hell of Catholic theology, for instance, would be provinces of the realm of matter: we need but follow the risen bodies on the Day of Judgment on their opposite journeys in order to discover these provinces empirically, and much more easily than Columbus discovered the New World: and a poet as saturated with modern physics as Dante was with the physics of Aristotle and Ptolemy might no less accurately conceive their topography. Human spirits would dwell in their proper bodies: and can we doubt that the angels and the godhead itself would be manifested sensibly, or intellectually by the order of many sensible things? Otherwise there would seem to be no meaning in assigning to them individual and separate existence, or a power to act upon our own souls and bodies.

In the same way all so-called spiritual or supernatural influences coming from other worlds come, if they come at all, from other parts of the realm of matter. Transmigrations, apparitions, grace, and any regular or proportionate efficacy in will, sacrifice or prayer, could be traced by an adequate physics from their source to their final manifestation; and every miracle, without prejudice to its moral purpose and spiritual interpretation, would be a natural process open to the eye of an enlightened science. The supernatural, if it exists, is the truly natural, the comprehensively physical. We should need but to shake ourselves loose from the cramp of mundane stupidity and prejudice, in order to move at ease, and with scientific insight, through that wider cosmos. An honest theology is a system of physics: not because it need confuse the spiritual with the instrumental, but because it surveys the whole field of action which may be instrumental to the spirit. If real, the supernatural is the source of nature; revelation and miracles simply disclose the existence of remoter or hidden powers dipping into our conventional world, and seeming to contradict its laws in order to manifest some more fundamental harmony. Indeed, miracles could not contradict natural laws if they were not forces in the same field: the alleged law contradicted was some hasty generalization, made in ignorance of just these cases, where the intervention of remoter influences changed the ordinary course of events.

It would be easy to protest that this habit of positing external substances is unspiritual, and therefore quite fatally leads to a hideous materialism, such as I am proposing: instead, we should see God in the joyful transformations of our inner being. Certainly, you may regard not God only but the whole realm of matter as a distinction which you make within your mind; but natural philosophy (which includes the discovery of any existing Gods) begins when you ask yourself on what occasions and under what conditions your precious self suffers these transmutations: and you could never answer that question without positing the realm of matter, doubtless under some other name. Nor is this really avoided by the resolute transcendentalists who refuse to admit any active principle save that of their own imagination: for the substance exorcised out of the natural world turns up here in the poet's heart. This groundless Will, Life, or Vital Impulse in him, what is it but the thinnest of rhetorical disguises for matter seething in his body? A great ambiguity remains in idealistic systems touching the distribution of this agent, whether it be deployed naturalistically in many persons and places, or confined to the solipsism of the thinking function in the speaker: but there is no ambiguity touching the brutally material nature of this agent, wherever it works: it is the principle of irrationality, energy, flux, and formless existence.

Although matter, then, is the only factor concerned in action, the idea of matter is far from being the only idea which contact with matter excites in the human organism. Any sensuous, verbal, or moral term will do, if it be used judiciously and instinctively discounted and translated into its material equivalent when, in action, we come to close quarters. Nevertheless the scientific value of any idea intended to describe substance, or to map for us the dynamic world, increases with the degree to which it specifies the local diversity, change, continuity, measure, and calculable behavior in that substance: in other words, with the degree in which it expresses substance in nakedly material terms. Everything else in human ideas is poetry and rhetoric, or literary psychology describing the equally redundant sensibility of kindred mortals; and this language, like this sensibility, is continually changing without more serious inconvenience than comes of changing the prevalent speech. Materialistic science is itself a language: he would be a sad materialist who took his notions of matter for matter itself. What is loosely called the utility of such ideas consists in the fact that they reflect—quite uselessly and intellectually—the form of highly useful actions—actions in which very accurate adjustments are made to surrounding matter through instruments and mechanical reckoning.

There is in such language—as in mathemathics, which is a chief part of it—a sort of bewildering and empty clearness; it records the methods of action, and a living being is happier when he acts spontaneously, without knowing how. Action itself, for a liberal mind, is only instrumental. Nevertheless, one of the uses of proficiency in action is to establish a critical materialism in the mind: not that such a picture is particularly beautiful, but it helps to clear away many an ancient confusion and equivocation, and frees the spirit for its proper function. The very images of sense, which are the first symbols for matter, are themselves liberated by a more sceptical materialism; and studied apart from their instrumental function, they become aesthetic objects on their own account and are honorably entertained by the spirit as celestial visitors or eternal essences. Similarly with all the hierarchy of notions that may complicate or replace the images of the senses: they are all essences essentially, an ultimate mathematical materialism being the most immaterial of them all. But any of them, and mathematical materialism most advantageously, may become a mask for material power, as my notions of my friend the boxer were, during the bout, my masks for his capacity of hitting and being hit. Thus, while action meets matter on its own ground with its own weapons, thought can picture matter in a thousand ways; and this intellectual fertility, besides pleasantly enlightening the spirit about its bonds with matter, may help to fill it with ideas fit for contemplation, and movements happy in themselves. When once the fear of making some wrong move is allayed, the heterogeneity of the signs we may use for matter is a poetic advantage, and the indirection of our intellectual contact with it a gain in liberty. Matter in us, being responsive to matter elsewhere, has a life which is relevant to things external: it can therefore reach knowledge, of a sort, about the realm of matter in general: but after all it is the matter within us that concerns us directly and is our proper life: and this is more generous and self-expressive when left free than when forced to be attentive to its outlying food or dangers. It is spontaneously directed on other realms of being rather than on the realm of matter to which, materially, it belongs.

There is indeed a natural hierarchy, an order of derivation and superposition among the four realms of being which I distinguish—and this is the reason for distinguishing them particularly. Other classifications might be just as convenient, and perhaps more obvious: but they would hardly mark such intrinsic diversities, and interrelations, in ontological levels. The realm of spirit is based on modes of matter, not on any material element taken separately: in other words, it is based on facts in the realm of truth. But truth means truth about existence; it means existence viewed under the form of eternity, in all its relations in the realm of essence. The distribution of matter determines all truths about it, and consequently all moral and mental facts. Yet matter itself could not exist if it possessed no essence and was not deployed into a system of changing relations themselves definite and possessing an essence: so that at the base of everything lies the eternal distinctness and variety of those forms which existence may wear and which may exist by exchanging.

MORAL SYMBOLS
IN THE BIBLE[1]

IN HONORING ME with an invitation to speak to you on a Biblical subject you must have been aware that I am no Biblical scholar: these things, as we say locally, are not in my department. A rumor may also have reached you—I won't say how well founded—that I am not altogether orthodox in theology; so that you are not expecting, perhaps, to hear me discourse on the authenticity of revelation or on the essential harmony between religion and science. Yet, in a sense, that is precisely my intention. By moral symbols in the Bible, I mean those spontaneous images or doctrines which transcribe there a genuine moral experience or a genuine moral ideal. If the Bible, when studied critically, seems a translation of moral truth into transparent

[1] In the margin of the original manuscript, Santayana has written: "Not read to the H. C. A. Oral and far milder version was substituted." I can only infer from this note that Santayana was reluctant to offend the religious susceptibilities of his audience. But I was unable to discover at Harvard what club or society the H. C. A. referred to. I do know, however, that this paper was composed about the time of *Interpretations of Poetry and Religion* (1900), as Santayana once told me that he later regretted not having included it in that early volume of essays. [D. C.]

symbols, there is at once established a fundamental harmony between its substance and reason; all that part of religious tradition which manifests this harmony is thereby justified and shown to be—apart from its mythical element—a vehicle for true wisdom.

If you open any ancient book, even the oldest in existence, you are at once confronted by a finished language, a multitude of assumed persons and things, a full-fledged pantheon, and a current morality. Thus history begins by plunging, like the approved epic, *in medias res*. We have no means of going further back; and in order to understand the background of the earliest records our one resource is to read on. Gradually the uses of words will reveal their acceptation: the persons named, by their attributions and conduct, will disclose their character; and we shall come to know the world we read of as we have in a measure unraveled the world in which we live, by gradual acquaintance and shrewd hypothesis. Every feature in an ancient document and in the life it describes is a symbol which we must endeavor to interpret. It is an expression the significance of which we have to reconstruct, a result the causes and meaning of which we have to discover.

In the Bible we find many such symbols standing for things easily recognized and familiar to every age: words for sun, moon, horse, bread, water. Yet even here much imaginative reconstruction is needed if we wish to *render* back to those names the full resonance they had in antiquity. Who but a poet could ever say what the moon was to the shepherds of Asia, or the horse or the well to men who lived in the desert? Yet these are symbols for physical things and for patent experiences. We have before us the harder task of interpreting other symbols—symbols for moral ideas, for piety and hope—which we find constantly employed in the Bible, without any explanation of their range and with meanings which, as they were always taken for granted, were probably never the same.

In religious thought and cultus, symbols for moral and physical things are often identical, and have consequently an ambiguous meaning. The Sabbath, for instance, if we look to its origin is based on sympathy with natural changes, on the instinct, if I may say so, to dance with the seasons: for the new-moons with which the Bible associates the Sabbath tell their own story, and the week is but the quarter of a lunar month. So far the Sabbath is a physical symbol; that is, it translates or celebrates the ways of nature in a human institution, and is one of man's efforts to salute and to express the world that surrounds him. This poetic and astronomic observance was no doubt overlaid with myths and superstitions, and soon acquired a new function. The Sabbath, being a day for worship, was a day for joy and rest; it was a day for sacrifice, which in the days of natural religion could not be severed from feast and frolic. So it became an institution that called a halt in the routine of life, suspended sordid occupations, gave occasion for happy intercourse, and, when religion grew soberer and more austere, for high communion. It became a day for searching the heart and drawing up one's accounts with the eternal. Thus the Sabbath became a moral symbol. It was a custom resting, for all men knew (since now the new-moons and country feasts were forgotten) merely on tradition and sheer authority; but in effect it had acquired a moral sanction, for it served a human and ideal end, and supported, in a great measure, man's spiritual existence.

By a moral symbol, then, I understand any practice, doctrine, or figure of speech, by which a moral interest is expressed and furthered: in other words, any religious tradition, whatever its hieratic origin, which serves to focus moral life and to define that living ideal which is implied in men's actual judgments and aspirations. Of many symbols of this nature to be culled from the Bible, I will select three, perhaps among the most important, for a brief explanation: namely the Law, the Covenant, and the Kingdom of Heaven.

The Hebrews never divided religion from civic life and their laws were a set of regulations embodying all tribal customs and duties. These laws were partly hygienic, partly political, partly moral, partly ceremonial. In its beginnings this body of usages seems not to have differed much from that of other Semite peoples; but when triumphs and misfortunes had come to heighten national feeling, and monotheism had been jealously established, observance of the law became not only the sign of national individuality and unity but also, as was believed, the means to national well-being and victory in war. Indeed, it was when Assyria loomed on the horizon that an explicit promulgation of the law, in a revised and far stricter form, seems to have occurred. Practices, some neglected, some never before established, but dictated now by the prophetic zeal beginning to stir the people's leaders, were proclaimed under Josiah to be the law of the land: a proclamation made, of course, under divine authority. In an age when every prophet could cry: "So saith the Lord," it could not seem illegitimate for the priests to declare: "So said Moses." Conscience, in a primitive and inspired people, often expresses itself in an apocryphal manner which conscience, in a critical age, would altogether exclude. It was then hardly conceivable that what was obviously right and necessary should not be the will of Jehovah, manifested of old to the fathers in the desert, and now again whispered in their children's hearts. To contrive a stricter observance was accordingly an act at once of experimental prudence—a means of making destiny, perhaps, less unfavorable—and an act of more fervent worship—a renewal of faith in Jehovah, to whose hands the nation's fortunes were thus entrusted more solemnly and completely than ever.

This experiment failed signally. Jerusalem was taken, the Temple destroyed, and the flower of the people carried into exile. The effect of failure, however, was not to discredit the Law, now once for all adopted by the unshakable Jews. On the contrary, when they returned from exile they re-established it with greater strictness than ever, adding all the minute observances, ritualistic and social, enshrined in Leviticus. It was in the ecclesiastical community thus formed that to meditate on the Law day and night and to observe the Lord's statutes became so sweet and pious an ideal to priest and Levite, and to their devout flock. It was then that the Psalmist could sing: "Lord, I have loved the habitation of thy house, and the place where thine honour dwelleth." Or again: "The Lord is my shepherd: I shall not want. He maketh me to lie down in green pastures; he leadeth me beside the still waters." This piety was fed on a sense at once of consecration and guidance. All was prescribed; and to fulfill the Law, just because it involved so complete and, as the world might say, so arbitrary a regimen, became a precious sacrifice of the will, a perpetual act of religion.

Religious dogmas show their worst side to the sceptic: for in his presence they feel bound to justify themselves literally. In making that attempt they obscure, under scientific and historical pretensions, whatever symbolic value and signification they may have had originally. Dogmas are at their best, on the contrary, when nobody denies them; for then their falsehood sleeps, like that of an unconscious metaphor, and their moral function is discharged instinctively. They count and are not defined, and the side of them which is not deceptive is the one that comes forward. So with the Hebrew Law. If you set it up against the scoffer as an actual divine enactment, you merely make him ask himself if you are dreaming awake. But in its day, when no one contradicted it, the Law was the form of an intense and isolated polity, enlisting in its service, as ancient polities did, every moral and imaginative function. The myth about its origin was comparatively harmless and even legitimate, because such was the only available method of expressing the Law's rational authority. What was condemnable in the Jews was not that they asserted the divinity of their own Law, for that they did with substantial sincerity and truth, but that they denied the divinity of other nation's laws and deities; for this they did not from critical insight or intellectual scruples but out of pure bigotry, conceit, and hatred. They did not want other nations also to have a God. No civilized people had had this audacity before. They all recognized one another's religions, if not as literally true (for some familiarity is needed to produce that illusion), certainly as more or less sacred and significant. Had the Jews not been guilty of this unprecedented arrogance, and taught Christians and Mohammedans that unhappy lesson, the nature of religion would not have been falsified among us, and we should not now have so much to apologize for and to retract.

What the Law did for the Jews in practice was to formulate moral obligation, and make the sense of it prominent and distinct. Moral obligation is something every being must feel who understands his natural interests and his natural conditions: for the conditions of man's life impose labor and restraint, and his natural interests lead to generosity and idealism. That the Hebrew Law was national rendered it even more specifically a moral bond. It constituted a brotherhood within which charity and mutual intelligence could flourish all the more intensely, in that a brutal and dogged hardness might still be shown towards the outer world. A small society has a great advantage in establishing discipline. Its influence is more penetrating and at the same time more welcome, for everyone has something tangible to hold to and his sacrifices bear visible fruit in a common life of which he shares the benefits.

It has been said that a retrogression took place in Jewish religion when instead of the prophets' insight, by which the most trifling conventions on a par with fundamental righteousness was identified with wise political and social action, the priests and Levites established a ritualistic Law, endowed with a literal and irrational authority, and put the most trifling conventions on a par with fundamental duties. It was necessary, we are told, that another Prophet should come to teach anew that to love one another was the true law, and thus to bring back religion from its dogmatic petrifaction to being a fluid and symbolic sanction for moral forces. The ultimate value of any law—and also of any sentiment, like love—lies of course in its eventual beneficence; and precepts, with the ideals they express, need to be constantly vivified by being readjusted to extant interests. The life prescribed by a revealed law may not be wiser or nobler than that which many a nation may lead without such a law, and a certain narrowness in sympathy and understanding will probably be involved in possessing any very definite institutions believed to be divine. The world has seen riper ethical systems than the Hebrew Law, presenting a better ideal of human life and mind. The Greeks, for instance, felt far more justly not only the basis and method of morals, but also its goal. Yet an established code, reputed divine, when reverenced and obeyed with scrupulous loyalty, has an important influence on character. A habit of obedience, the constant sense of supervision and responsibility, awe before a command that being immutable imposes itself regardless of all particular circumstances, and yet, being essentially wise, generally rewards the obedient with ultimate advantages, or at any rate with a sense of duty fulfilled amid the commendation of the faithful—this is an inestimable moral power. The Greeks, for all their wisdom, were impotent to realize or maintain their ideals so soon as meddlesome sophists and opportunists began to relax the statutes established by ancient legislators. So needful is a steady discipline and a sense of absolute attachment to a common ideal if even the wisest laws are to be practically fruitful. Thus it has come to pass that out of Hebraic legality has come Hebraic puritanism, and out of puritanism has come, not indeed moral wisdom, but moral strength. Discipline is a vicarious reason and teaches people to act on principle. In morals as in war, the readiness is much. When a man is girded for action, willing to take infinite pains, capable of co-operation with others, trustworthy, and loyal, he is good material for a state. Nothing is needed but a great opportunity, the revelation of something noble and truly deserving to be done for such a man to become a master in action. So we observe in this country a great moral heritage surviving from an age of moral constraint; we find a sense for conduct, a love of labor, a gift for organization, which after creating farms has created constitutions, and then colleges and navies, and which, if a richer experience leaves its strength unimpaired may yet create a noble happiness to justify navies and colleges, constitutions and farms.

If the Law was a school of fidelity and stood for obligation, there was another Hebrew tradition which expressed another side of moral life, namely, its conditions. The Covenant, stated in its crudest mythical terms, was a contract made between Jehovah and his people, whereby he would insure their prosperity so long as they obeyed his commandments. Literally taken this doctrine involves all that is most objectionable in Hebraism: the notion that there was a specially chosen people, that a national deity was the only God, that divine commandments were arbitrary, and that an arbitrary material reward would follow obedience to them. There is no need, however, to interpret the Covenant in such an unintelligent fashion, especially as the Prophets, who have the best right to speak in the matter, penetrated boldly to the moral truth enveloped in the parable. Their procedure in this case is a model for all religious reformers. They did not deny the dogma; they did not fight against verbal usage; they accepted the medium of half-conscious allegory in which religion must move. They made themselves the spokesmen of orthodoxy: but they re-interpreted orthodoxy so as to restore to it its radical significance: they fulminated rational truths in the language and on the authority of inspiration. In the first place, in respect to the protection which Jehovah dispensed to his people, this was, they said, no foregone favoritism, such that whatever the Jews should do, if they cried, "Lord, Lord," and performed the appointed sacrifices, they should be safe. Far from it. Jehovah's protection was conditional and his affection for Israel was reversible and far from blind. The condition of safety was right conduct.

Right conduct, moreover, was no matter of priestly prescription; it was a matter of conscience and of the natural laws of life. Sacrifices, if made a substitute for efficacious action, were an abomination. The prophets, indeed, did not conceive right conduct in its widest political aspects: they conceived it mainly as private virtue, as justice and love. Yet justice and love are great bulwarks for a state, and to say that God would reward them in the arena of international life was no oracle heard in a dream: it was an observed law. The conception of God's commandments was thus lifted into a moral conception, while the notion of God's arbitrary patronage was purified into a conditional favor shown to desert. The Covenant became again a moral symbol: for of course, in the beginning, it had been nothing else. It had come at first to give a religious sanction to human enactments, as now it became a religious expression for universal laws. The Jews were fervent: their civic life was concentrated and intense, they were brought during the Prophets' time into collision with formidable empires; and thereby the general conditions of social existence, which a sleepy philosophy may trace in a desultory fashion through the pages of history, loomed before them with terrible definiteness and prompted the sublime eloquence of their prophets. Never has religion united so much zeal with so much practical wisdom; never have its oracles been so unmistakably moral symbols.

I have said that the virtues the prophets commended were private; they were not virtues which in themselves could maintain a nation against military and political forces far greater than its own. Israel succumbed: but its private virtues gave the remnant of that state a novel power, and made it the religious teacher of the world. The promised land was lost; but in its place Israel inherited the kingdom of heaven. Here is a new moral symbol, the expression of a new spiritual life.

In the last three centuries before the Christian era religion suffered a great transformation in the whole western world, a transformation which Christianity afterwards summed up and consolidated, but which it was very far from having begun. Ancient religions—Jewish and pagan alike—had been civic and national; and whatever in them went beyond those limits had been naturalistic myth. But now civic life, for one cause or another, had died out everywhere. The state had become an administration, the arts a memory, the army a profession, the cultus a traditional pageant. Cosmopolitan Rome had destroyed manly piety, the symbol of national and family life, and opened the door to a brooding religiosity and to every stray superstition. The individual stood alone in the world and could find little that was sacred in the unnatural void that seemed to separate his soul from heaven.

As the Jews had been most passionate in their civic religion, while Canaan or Jerusalem still seemed a promised land, so they were most profound in their spirituality, now that earthly ambitions began to lose their ascendancy. The Law and the temple-worship had been their first consolation; and we have seen how the Psalms gave voice to the chastened and lyric piety which flourished in the courts of that national sanctuary, half fortress and half cloister. But such an existence, after all, was pathetic and meager:

the attitude of expectation which the Jews had always cultivated could not be abandoned now. They lived in their poverty and dispersion as in a limbo from which some messiah would come to summon them again to life. But to what life? The whole problem of religion now lay in that question. The busy fanatical burghers might become Pharisees, and think of a new kingdom to be established by miracle, more powerful than Rome's was, and more gorgeous than they imagined Solomon's to have been. The Hellenizers at Alexandria might wander into metaphysics and turn the earnest piety of their race into cosmic romances. But between an orthodoxy that was not so historical, perhaps, as it thought itself, and an alien gnostic speculation, Hebrew religion could find a third course, at once responsive to sad experience and to the age's need, a movement which transferred the nation's hopes and fidelity into a new sphere. This was the direction taken by the Essenes, by John the Baptist, and finally by Christ himself. It involved a complete spiritualization of Hebraism; it prophesied the Kingdom of Heaven.

The antecedents of this watch-word are easy to trace; to render its exact ultimate meaning is a more difficult matter. What Canaan had been to migrating Israel and Jerusalem to Israel in exile, that a restored kingdom had since become to all the Jews. Ezechiel had already so described the New Jerusalem that it was a miraculous city, impossible to realize in Judea, and well-nigh celestial. Only a short step separated his Temple, with its choirs and trumpeters and adoring multitudes marshalled around, from what we call heaven. Especially is the transition easy, when we remember that the righteous were expected to rise again at the great day when the Messiah should appear, and to enjoy for ever the good things of the new dispensation. The kingdom of heaven, in its literal sense, means this supernatural regimen, which after a thundering cataclysm, was to be established on the ruins of the heathen world.

To this image, to this traditional dream, the glad tidings of the Gospel are associated: but you will agree with me, I am sure, when I say that here the vehicle is not identical with the meaning it conveys, and that, in the mouth of Jesus, the kingdom of heaven is a moral symbol. The pictorial vehicle is indeed extraordinarily appropriate. The contrast it sets up between two successive worlds is the graphic image of that contrast which the Gospel everywhere makes between the two ways of living, of loving and esteeming everything—the earthly way, which is to be discarded, and the spiritual way, which is to be pursued. In the Beatitudes, in the Lord's Prayer, in those parables in which the kingdom of heaven is illustrated by various analogies, we learn of no historic catastrophe, of no future prosperous existence; we learn rather the economy of spiritual life, its inner fruits, its mystic judgments, its ideal consolations. The kingdom of heaven is within us: that is the sum of the matter. It is a new principle of estimation by which the passions are silenced, the motive for wrongdoing and for harsh judgment is removed, anxiety is dissipated, vanities laid aside, and suffering relieved or accepted. This principle is mystical: it involves being born again and reversing all natural impulses. In contrast to human enmities and censoriousness it may be called love; for it seeks nothing for itself and forgives everything in others. In contrast to political or industrial efforts, it may be called detachment and unworldliness. In contrast to natural passions, it may be called asceticism. In contrast to the Jewish Law, it may be called inwardness, liberty, directness of insight and spiritual autonomy. In contrast to the whole public and current movement of the world, it may be called religion itself. It is a disenchantment full of light and consolation; a self-surrender full of peace; an isolation rich in the sense of union with all things and with their principle.

Has the kingdom of heaven, as proposed in the Gospel, become wholly a moral symbol, or does it involve the announcement of a miraculous external revolution? Are the meek blessed because they shall literally inherit the earth, i.e., because the mighty are about to be put down from their seats and those of low degree to be exalted? Or are the meek blessed only because, by being meek, they are masters of all ambitions and vanities and inherit all material things, to use them as God's gifts rather than as coveted possessions? I cannot venture to express an opinion on the point: it would require the finest historical judgment to say whether no shade of millennianism remained imbedded in these calls to a new life; an element which might afterwards be brought forward again by the more materializing disciples. But it is certain that such millennianism, if it existed at all, was largely submerged, and that the image of a new world was used to express the advent of a new moral dominion over actual experience.

As Spinoza, who was the first of Biblical critics in many respects, pointed out long ago, metaphor plays a part in Oriental thought which we in the West are not accustomed to, and our tendency is to take literally what is meant figuratively, rather than to put too much meaning and too much poetry into what we read. And so I feel sure that we should be safe in reading this metaphor of the kingdom of heaven in the most ideal possible sense. It may have had other significations clinging to it also; but these prophetic and earthly hopes were taken in the gospel as a point of departure, as something to transform and turn into an illustration for the genuine inward salvation, for the change of heart which makes the world different without changing its ancient and predestined ways. Otherwise the blessedness of hungering and thirsting, of being meek and pure in heart, would be provisional only: as soon as the cataclysm came humility and persecution would cease to be blessed. We cannot think the new life of the Gospel was a transitional regimen, a morality to which another morality—quite opposite in character—was to succeed in a few years. Such an interpretation savors too much of back-sliding: it is too clearly a reversion from the Cross to the dream of sitting upon thrones and judging the twelve tribes of Israel.

The Gospel, in conceiving the kingdom of heaven in a mystic and, if you like, an ascetic sense, in conceiving it as a life of insight and union with God's will, put forward an ideal which every age will not accept with equal enthusiasm. As the Law was a symbol for *method in life*, as such method could be embodied by an ancient theocratic people, isolated and ignorant; as the Covenant was a symbol for the *conditions of life*, so far as the same people could discover them; so the Kingdom of Heaven was a symbol for *life in the ideal*, as that people, after a long political decadence, could finally conceive it. We must remember that the Jews, even in their palmy days, had not possessed anything which, in the occidental sense, can be called government, science, or art. They had no liberal interests for the ideal to express. They had only elementary human experience—the perpetual round of Oriental piety and servitude, in the bosom of a scorched and exhausted country. When a chastened spiritual eye surveyed such an existence, it could find nothing in it to idealize except the sentiment it provoked. In such a world a wholly purified and disillusioned religion, such as Christ's was, could teach men only to succor the afflicted, to understand and forgive the sinful, to pass through the sad pageant of life unspotted and resigned, placing all their dignity and rapture in a large humility and a mystic union with the unseen. There is no hint in the Gospel that the mind or the hand of man can ever construct anything; and Christianity —before Greeks and Romans and Teutons had made Christendom out of it—was a religion of pure sentiment, of disposition alone. It contained no formative principle to govern intellect or institutions; it preached nothing but the kingdom of heaven.

This partiality in the experience on which the kingdom of heaven was to rest, was no obstacle to the perfect idealization to which it subjected that experience. As in every age man needs a method of life, so that the Law is a symbol of eternal validity; as in every age, too, conditions of life have to be recognized, so that a covenant with them has to be observed; so in every age, at every turn of action and thought, experience suggests its own ideal, by which alone it can be judged; so that a kingdom of heaven has to be preached to all nations. Were no ideal conceived at all, men would be the horses harnessed to their own chariot, docile perhaps and hard-working, but neither knowing where they go, nor indeed going anywhere. All life in the world is also, if rational, life in the ideal; and what the kingdom of heaven was to the spiritualized Jews, the eternalized beauty and goodness of things—where they are really beautiful and good—may be to every man passing through existence. We need not, perhaps, in this age and country, surrender so many ambitions as the Gospel assumes must be surrendered by a spiritual man; we may find other avenues to the highest good as well as inward detachment and charity. To purity of life and sentiment we may hope to add dominion of the outer world, to make it also ideal. Yet after all, the limits of human life and art are soon reached, and renunciation, wherever it may set in, must set in somewhere, to stretch from that point to infinity. The kingdom of this world, however improved, is still transitory and full of sorrow; and it will always be glad tidings to know that the kingdom of heaven is at hand. Even in the midst of action, and sometimes by virtue of its very intensity and restlessness, the liberating word is heard gladly: "Behold the lilies of the field . . ." "Thy sins are forgiven thee . . ." "This day thou shalt be with me in paradise." The Bible, by including among its moral symbols a kingdom which is not of this world, has engrossed a great chapter in man's spiritual history and appealed, as it would not otherwise have done, to thousands of souls.

What the kingdom of heaven was is still an ultimate ideal. The world and the flesh are full of blindness, injustice, and contradiction: and yet the elementary cravings that lead men into so much vanity and mutual injury are innocent in themselves. Mortal errors deserve to be forgiven. Some sinners have loved much: others know not what they do. The spectacle of existence in every age and clime is fit to awaken the feelings with which Jesus surveyed it—love and sorrow and a high detachment. Experience is beautiful at its springs—the kingdom of heaven belongs to little children, for their fugitive ideal is not yet crossed, and their ingenuous action is not yet odious. But experience is horrible in its entanglements. Nations and churches and philosophies are whited sepulchres—disguised betrayals of their primitive intent. These entanglements, however, are unstable; the very contradiction which makes them horrible destroys them inwardly; and where there is no justice and no peace there is also no permanence.

What shall we say remains in this perpetual destruction of perpetual evil? The answer is experience of this divine judgment and knowledge of the ideal intent which those fickle existences expressed and forthwith betrayed. There is a creative undying force that grafts an ideal on every natural equilibrium; there is a soul in every body and in every creature an angel that sees the face of God. To salute that angel, to understand that soul, to love the suffering world so much that we can see through its miseries the ideal of what it meant to be—that is to live in the spirit, in the presence of the ideal and the eternal. This ideal is the will which we must pray may be done on earth, even as in heaven, its native dwelling. It shines in eternal perfection: to this parent good, from which our goodness flows, we must turn for our standard and our solace: to its immortal energies, incessantly reincarnated, we must resign our spirit, when we can express our spirit no more.

The Bible and the doctrines which the Church has evolved out of it have a double value and a double kind of validity. Their moral validity lies in their adequacy as symbols of human experience; their physical validity lies in their literal truth in describing historical or metaphysical facts. In calling the Law, the Covenant, and the Kingdom of Heaven moral symbols, I am not discussing or prejudging the question whether they are not also, at least in some measure, descriptions of material beings. The Bible unquestionably contains a great deal of history, and some metaphysics may be extracted from it also, with enough good will and determination. In the supernatural nothing is impossible and those conceptions which, in point of origin and ideal value, are undoubtedly moral symbols, may be also descriptions of positive fact. A material Jehovah might have given the Law to Moses written out upon stone tables: he might have made a *viva voce* contract with Israel, and proceeded to exercise the legal rights so acquired; and the upper sky may contain an assembly of transfigured persons to be reached by following the angels up Jacob's ladder, or by simply dying quietly in your bed. We may grant anything to exist for which anybody thinks he has found evidence. If you imagine, however, that the supernatural, by existing, acquires any moral authority or any religious value, you have not duly considered the subject. A material God might issue laws, but why should I obey them? If he threatens me with punishment, it will be his ministers of vengeance that I should have to recognize, not his will. Now God's ministers are the objects of experience. If I have squared my accounts with these, I have settled my practical relations with everything supernatural behind them. A material God is therefore important or discoverable only in so far as he acts materially: his further existence, that action being given, makes no difference in his authority. But perhaps the laws coming from a supernatural source may be premonitions or expressions of my own conscience and moral interests; so that in recognizing and obeying those laws I am furthering my own life. In that case, while the supernatural lawgiver may be an independent fact, his moral authority is a derivative symbol: for I recognize his goodness and the sanctity of his commands, only because I discover in them an expression of my ideal. The question of material existence, therefore, though most interesting in history and physics, and affecting morals, as historical and physical facts do, by modifying the conditions of action, is absolutely irrelevant to the inner principle of morals and of religion. Existences are objects for scientific judgment; and whether Jehovah really appeared on Mount Sinai, or made a covenant with Abraham, or holds a court in heaven into which, in a few years, you and I may hope to be admitted, are questions to be decided by historical good sense and empirical probability. Their solution affects spiritual life only by defining the environment in which spiritual life is to be led. While the New Jerusalem, for instance, was a worldly ideal, to be realized in Judea in the near future, it encouraged certain sentiments and efforts which were entirely discountenanced as soon as the New Jerusalem was sublimated into the kingdom of heaven; for now, the empirical prophecy being roundly reduced to a moral symbol, all preparations for the morrow were condemned as ignoble and childish, and the kingdom of heaven was said to have come already, and to be within the heart. Afterwards, however, the avowed symbol was in its turn understood to report an external fact, and to prophesy a metamorphosis of experience following upon death. So long as this supernatural vista represents and emphasizes things morally true—while your religious images, in becoming dogmas, do not cease to be moral symbols—no vitiation of conscience or of effort is involved. The result has even some emotional advantage, in as much as what at any rate would be an ideal is thought to have an actual embodiment somewhere in the universe. Thus if a born painter learns that Zeuxis and Apelles, who might hitherto have stood in his mind merely for ideal excellence in his art, were once actual men, and that their paintings gave immense pleasure to the Greeks, he will certainly be very glad to hear it. He may even be encouraged in his own work by knowing that others have succeeded. His ideal, however, and his possible success will remain his own. The news about Zeuxis and Apelles will not teach him how to paint, nor will it make his painting worth while in a sense in which it would not be equally worth while if Zeuxis and Apelles had never existed. So it is with supernatural events and supernatural beings. If you can credibly learn that they are actual and perfectly illustrate your ideals, that is an interesting and propitious discovery. But their dignity and authority continue to be derived from the ideal you have yourself constructed and which you believe them to realize so well. You would not for a moment admit their right to legislate for you if what they commanded or encouraged were wrong in your eyes. A revelation which did not express the mind and conscience of those to whom it was made, a revelation that favored immorality and misery, would be no religious revelation, but a sad discovery in history or science. The whole religious function of supernatural beings comes, then, from the fact that the idea of them is a moral symbol. Their whole authority is and remains rooted in this moral symbolism, in this expression they give to human ideals, whether they be also matters of fact, or only poetic expressions of experience and of the laws by which experience is governed. If any part of the hidden reality realizes what is my ideal now, the notion of that reality can serve me now for a moral symbol and be an object of religion. To discover that part of reality would interest and encourage me, because it would express my present aspiration. From this aspiration, which it would share with me, it would borrow its relevance and divinity. All the rest of the hidden or supernatural world, being ideally irrelevant to my present life, might be dismissed with a blessing, as we might dismiss the early Japanese heroes, or the salamanders that may at this moment be disporting themselves in Sirius. Whatever in religion and metaphysics is not a moral symbol is but physical speculation: it concerns the religious mind only in so far as it yields information about the conditions of action and happiness. It has only physical relations to the soul, being alien to it in intent and aspiration. It holds no communion with the spirit, for spirits can only unite by envisaging the same objects and pursuing the same ideals.

If therefore you have any suspicion that, in talking of moral symbols and in wishing to transfer the center of religious thought from dogma to idealization, I am juggling with words, or offering you a stone for bread or when you ask for a fish giving you a serpent, I beg you to reconsider the matter. You will find the exact opposite to be the case. Dogma is the indigestible stone: false physics, vitiating your conscience and deceiving you about the conditions of action, is the insidious serpent. It was against such religious materialism—such substitution of imaginary facts for moral symbols—that all the prophets, and Christ above all, were perpetually fighting. The hypostasis of moral symbols is an advantage when it is empirically justified and when it therefore does not traduce the actual facts or misrepresent the forces amidst which moral life actually develops. But if a man, in hypostasizing his ideals, so as to give them a greater emotional emphasis and definition, so conceives the world as to misrepresent the consequences which actually attend conduct, and to tamper with its real sanctions, he takes a grave responsibility. He is not only deceiving the intellect, which at best, perhaps, is tentative and symbolic in its representations, but he is vitiating the conscience. He is disorganizing life and leading men away from discipline and wisdom. Such a procedure is what we call superstition or else fanaticism— superstition when it is merely ignoble and idle, fanaticism when it is positively malignant. Superstition and fanaticism have often been allied with religion or have even taken its place. They are now, in their extreme forms, generally reprobated. I would ask you, however, to consider whether you still regard the principle of superstition and fanaticism as the principle of true religion. If so, you make what you call religion detestable to every rational mind, to every one who has at heart the progress and happiness of the spirit.

Nothing avails, I know, against congenital inclination and inveterate tradition. In vain will you use the plainest words, declaring that God is a spirit and that those that worship him must worship him in spirit and in truth. No one will understand you. Your earnest disciples, thinking to defend your memory, will proceed to explain that you meant that God has no hands and no feet but is a quite bodiless psychological combination of will and idea. It is almost useless to protest: when instinct leads men into such courses it is not likely that argument should hold them back. They will continue to turn truths into existences and expressions into myths; and if by a great effort, and at the cost of being called an atheist and condemned to death, you persuade them to surrender an ancient misunderstanding and to see, in the old symbols, the meaning they possessed, your hard-won victory will avail nothing. Your followers will turn your own words into a new mythology, and the spirit you preached about will itself have become a thing. In the ways of men, as in nature, there is sometimes a pertinacity that strikes one dumb. It is impossible to refute a fable; but it is also unnecessary. That may safely be left to its friends. If you would understand spiritual religion, disassociate yourselves altogether from controversy. Turn rather to human nature, to poetry, to history, to the Bible which contains so much of all three. Read it not with superstitious qualms and selfish anxiety. Read it with an open heart, with a humane imagination. Remember that religion must have meant something when it was first conceived. It was then, beyond question, a sort of symbols for human experience. Try to conceive what that experience was, and make yourself free, by that comprehension, to use the same symbols, or others like them, to express your own soul. Do not be led aside from this task of self-knowledge and idealization into physical dogmas, which too often betray the interest they pretend to support, and inspire nothing but a rabid desire to deceive and to be deceived. Clear your mind of these vapors. Morality is the most natural thing in the world, and only one who sees things as they are can have a pure religion. If you can restore the imagination to its rights and recover that ingenuous experience and confidence out of which religion has grown up, you will feel a wonderful clearness and homeliness pervading the subject. All the prophets will become intelligible. Not one inspired voice will ring hollow, miraculous, or false. In the most oracular sayings you will discover an honest meaning, something quite obvious to him who spoke it and very likely to be drawn afresh from your own experience. You will converse with the highest minds as if you were school-fellows talking together, and when you least think of it deep will answer unto deep.

THE COMING PHILOSOPHY

THE FOLLOWING PAGES, though some controversial strains
may run through them, are inspired on the whole by a
sense of pleasure and relief. I have read Professor E. B.
Holt's book on *The Concept of Consciousness* and I have
understood it. At least I think so; and if the sequel should
prove the contrary, I hope the author or his friends will
admonish me publicly or privately. Impotence to understand the new American philosophy has weighed upon me
for years. The trouble could hardly lie in any want of
sympathy on my part with the general direction of the
school nor (what is a great bond) with its aversions; indeed, my *Life of Reason* was taken in some quarters for a
contribution to the movement. Could I have become afflicted so soon with the intellectual deafness of age? Or
were the new developments of the school so profound and
so scientific as to baffle my ignorance and superficiality?
There may be something in each of these explanations;
but now that after long and painful efforts I feel I have
overcome the difficulty, I do not hesitate to say that it lay
chiefly in this—that the new American philosophy (a
fusion of transcendentalism, pragmatism, immediatism, and

logical realism) is itself perplexed by confused thinking, half-meant, random assertions, undigested traditions, uncouth diction, and words turned from their right use. Never was a group of thinkers so sophisticated and so ill-educated; Greek sophistry was perverse, but it was skillful; medieval scholastic language was barbarous, but it was plain. "It is said," Mr. Holt writes (p. 313), "that a third [theory] has been devised by Dewey, which I regret my inability to discuss because after careful perusal of the words I have been unable to gather a connected meaning." Now what has happened to Mr. Holt with one of his colleagues has happened to me with most of them, and in a lesser measure with Mr. Holt himself: not that his style is at all better, but that his wits are sharp, he leans on logic and physics more unequivocally, and above all he carries his doctrines out boldly to their extreme consequences, and so relieves us of the suspicion that he might not have meant in the beginning what he seemed to say.

The fundamental thesis is this: that consciousness is nothing but its immediate objects, which are all exactly what they would be if no one was conscious of them. These objects are of every sort—terms, propositions, sensible qualities, relations, values, emotions. They are all universals, that is, they are all capable of being repeated without losing their identity; and the only sense in which they may become particular is that, when repeated in a determinate context, the object so individuated can not be repeated again, unless, indeed, the whole context is repeated; so that (unless the world goes round in cycles) each fact in it is particular although, when abstracted from its context, it remains a universal still, and is identical with all the other instances of it that may be found in other contexts. When any of these beings—say the disc of the full moon—comes under observation, it enters a mental context which is more limited than the context it has in the mathematical and even in the material world; but in all three worlds it remains the same identical universal being, and there is no sense in supposing that it is sometimes a mathematical disc, sometimes a material disc, and sometimes a psychic disc in its nature. It is always that being the entire nature of which is simply to be a disc—a logical or essential disc if you will; and this identical being when it appears in the evolution of nature is a disc materialized, and when it appears in consciousness is a disc perceived; not that these are two different sorts of disc, but the same universal disc in different contexts.

An implication of this view, which Mr. Holt is far from deprecating, is that no being is intrinsically logical, psychic, or material, but that each may enter any of these fields, so that feelings and purposes may be a part of natural objects, wooden tables and multiplication tables may be parts of the mind, and equations and laws may be parts of both mind and matter; while mind and matter, with all that is in them, remain parts of the realm of logical or neutral being. A point, or the binomial theorem, is nothing essentially mathematical or ideal; it may be a physical and existential element, and indeed material things are composed of nothing but universals of one sort or another, evolving in accordance with some formula itself abstract and universal. Even thought is not essentially mental, for it is nothing but the objects thought of—triangles, trees, people—and these miscellaneous objects may lie perfectly well in nature and grow, at the same time that they appear in consciousness and are noticed. Pleasure itself is not essentially psychic. When it is felt it is brought within consciousness, but it may lie unnoticed in the movement and relations of things. The roses that blush unseen do not waste their fragrance, because fragrance is pleasant in itself and can not be wasted; it may merely be missed, and not figure in the sensations of a dull passer-by. What defines the psychic field, and raises what lies within it to the conscious power, is the response of the nervous system; a response which may be to anything embodied in the environment, at any distance of time or space, and, of course, among other things, to beauties, purposes, and all other values supposed to be essentially immaterial, but really as truly embodied in matter as are mathematical volumes and velocities. Memories and fancies are simply remote or abstract elements of nature to which the nervous system is responding. Furthermore, errors exist in the absence of opinion. The mere apprehension of some neutral being is not an error, nor can any term be false in itself. But when a formula begins to be expressed in a series of facts, that formula is equivalent to the proposition that it *is* so expressed, and to the purpose that it shall be; and if a contrary formula, also in operation, requires different facts to express it at the same point of time and place, one or both must be disavowed by the facts and must fail; and the one that fails will be an error. When we are deceived it is merely that one of these ill-fated propositions actually afloat in the world has come within our hypnotic view. It is a little failure in creation that our errors register and are, as if we registered and were a failure in the Stock Exchange.

This system is an immense simplification, and I can well imagine the sigh of relief and exultation with which the distracted pupil of modern philosophy might greet it. Art remains long, however, in spite of the impatience of genius, and we are not at the end of the story.

It is to be observed—for it is a sign of the times—that the system is confident and ambitious. "We shall one day learn that all being is a single, infinite, deductive system in which the entire variety develops deductively from a relatively small number of fundamental propositions" (p. 164). The aim is not to put together a personal system of philosophy, judicial, imaginative, religious, but rather to discover the system which is in the universe. Such is the aim of science, although scientific men may be less conscious of it and less prone than philosophers to anticipate the total system that might come to light in the end. When philosophers try to be scientific they are apt to fall into metaphysics—I mean into the abuse of making central and generative of the whole universe some principle peculiar to a particular field, in which personally they are most at home; so that their scientific philosophies are personal, after all. Hence the saying of Pascal that the principles of the philosophers are all true, but their systems false, because the contrary principles are true also. Mr. Holt will have it that propositions generate things and that deduction dominates evolution. Now this is pretty plainly an abuse

183

of logic and a reversion to a Platonic sort of metaphysics. The new logic is no doubt better than the old; it is mathematical instead of grammatical, and it leans on a more thorough and loving study of nature, discerning forms of change—processes, laws, equations—which, in fact, are woven far more intimately and lastingly into the structure of nature than are the plastic types, zoological and moral, on which the ancients doted. But forms of change are not changes, any more than ideals of man are men. To identify definitions with things and deduce existence from ultimate dialectical elements is gnostic procedure; and Mr. Holt's ontological hierarchy has a strangely gnostic air. Here it it, in abridgment:[1] identity, difference, number, the negative, logico-mathematical entities, forms of order, algebras innumerable, secondary qualities, intensity, geometry, higher mathematics, space, time, motion, mass, mechanics, physics entire, chemistry, material things, life, sciences of life (like paleontology), consciousness, psychology, anthropology, history, value.

Before we reach time in this chain of beings we are in the eternal, and although Mr. Holt makes propositions identical with forces and deduction identical with causation (for a realist with the motto that "everything is what it is and not something else" he identifies a good many things) it is clear that in the timeless the only procession possible, like that of the persons of the Trinity, will be by way of essential complement or explication, without creation or change. Of course if we begin by taking a pregnant proposition we shall find that others "follow"; but

[1] Page 155 ff.

the succession and the difference between synthesis and analysis lie in our method of survey; in the object there is only a mutual implication of elements, since it is out of time, as our survey is not. Again, until we reach space and material things, various propositions or purposes can not meet in conflict or meet at all, unless they involve one another. How in the eternal menagerie shall identity devour difference, or intensity sting and drive off the algebras innumerable, all of which must remain what they are? The superexistential is a happy family. If the eternal is to suffer it must become incarnate, and a mortal mother must be found for the child. Facts are transformations of previous facts, by which new qualities, themselves changeless, come to take the place of others, perhaps very like them, so that the transition is, or seems, continuous; but these qualities are not facts on their own account, pre-existing and coming together in space, like so many atoms, to compose the new being; they are connected by no external relations of genesis, position, or date, but only by those essential relations which must bind them always. I am not so rash as to deny that an algebraic expression exists for succession —the order of an irreversible manifold in one dimension, or something of that sort; but the fertility described by that formula or any other is not its own, but that of things; else the formula, which is a timeless being, would have tended to breed its material expression always and everywhere from all eternity: and as the negative would have been equally omnipresent and active, creation would have been stifled in the womb and there would be nothing but a perpetual and universal inhibition of every formula by every other. The initial bias of matter, accident, or brute existence unequally distributed must first give logic its foothold in time and place, if deductive evolution is to be set rolling; it must supply a groundless arbitrary premise of fact from which local and real consequences may follow. Mr. Holt's metaphysics is too Platonic; it leaves us in the air.[2]

The whole timeless prologue to creation is, therefore, useless for deducing those material objects which, according to Mr. Holt, make up consciousness when the nervous system responds to them; but it is not useless altogether, because without it we should not understand how consciousness catches sight of many things which are apparently not parts of the material environment. If, however, material things are themselves compounded of immaterial elements, any proposition they justify or any appearance they present may be an integral part of them, and, therefore, of the consciousness of them, when one arises. The devil, for instance, sometimes appears or is thought of, and yet, perhaps, is not one of the material irritants of

[2] There is, indeed, a very different metaphysical system adumbrated in the new philosophy; a temporal mechanism of qualitative existent elements, *minima sensibilia* and *intelligibilia,* which should foregather, like the atoms of Anaxagoras or the perceptions of Hume, into images and processes. Logistic theory would be driven, I suspect, to such a mechanism of immediate data, if it realized the impossibility of deducing a flux from timeless terms and timeless propositions. But this would be to abandon the courageous metaphysical conceptualism of Mr. Holt, who thinks the concept of flux is a flux in person; it would be to push nominalism into the heart of mathematics, maintaining (as I understand Mr. Bertrand Russell now does) that only the instances of anything (of numbers, for example) have any kind of being whatever, while as for universals, like the numbers themselves, they can be only predicates, and "it is a fallacy even to mention them."

the nervous system; but if the devil is a part of the negative, as he says in *Faust* that he is, he will turn out to have
been always a component element of nearly everything
on earth; and consciousness, being a cross-section of things
on earth, may very easily strike that negative vein in the
quartz, and catch the silhouette of Satan in any thing.
Unfortunately there are things which it is harder to make
room for in the outer world than for the principle of negation. Suppose I am at sea, a prey to mounting nausea,
and at the same time intent on the cruel, insultingly blue
vault of heaven. Where, in the environment, is this cruel
vault, this insulting blue, and this restless feeling? We
might agree on all hands that these things are nowhere,
if we consider their intrinsic being; the immediate data of
experience need have no place in nature—they may be
homeless and unattached, like some heaven of music or
religion. Yet Mr. Holt maintains, I hardly see on what
evidence, that no being appears to consciousness unless it
is actually an integral element, however formal, of the
environment to which the nervous system is responding;
and the nervous system, he admits, is nothing but a material mechanism responding to a material world. It follows
that the vault, the blue, the cruelty, the insult, and the
nausea, are integral elements in the scene of my voyage.
The nausea travels, I suppose, from the unhappy waves
(for the pathetic fallacy is obvious and sober truth for
this system) through the decks into the stomach. The
vault is presumably a cross-section of the atmosphere; but
is it forty miles high, or lower, and at what distance does
it sink into the sea? Does the blue color lie on this vault

only, as I seem to see it, or does it pervade the air? And are the cruelty and insults there chronically, or only when the seasick passenger passes unheeded beneath? In any case it is a relief to remember that these self-subsisting qualities and feelings, though exactly what we feel, subsist unfelt; the waves are not conscious of their inherent nausea, and the blue sky meets them at the horizon all unseen. In another place Mr. Holt condemns the notion of the subconscious; there may be as much forgotten or unrecovered consciousness as we choose, but there can be no unconscious or subconscious consciousness. I should agree to that; but is not an unfelt feeling much the same thing? Are we not confusing logical character with natural existence, essences with facts? The neutral and timeless being of nausea, insults, cruelty, concavity, and blue is possible being only; it is the ideal or description of how these things would look if they were seen, or what form they would possess if they existed. This unchangeable essence of each of them is quite independent of consciousness, but it is equally independent of waves, sky, ships, stomachs, eyes, and the whole flux of existence. What, I pray, is a nausea, or a cruelty, or an insult, or a landscape, which is not merely the character these things would have when perceived, but is an integral unperceived element in the actual material world? In general, what is the meaning of a nervous system *responding* to a secondary quality, a feeling, a proposition, or anything but a motion? Are we not being buffeted by a maddening perversion of language? Of course the reaction will vary with the quality of the motion that provokes it, and if, speaking in a way at once pedantic and slovenly, we say that a formula for motion *is* a motion, and that the sort of motion the nervous system reacts on when we see blue *is* blue, we may proclaim that the nervous system reacts on the formula and the color as given in consciousness. But it is a forced generalization to conclude, because in the case of gross contacts we look for what actually touches us, that in all cases we are conscious of all our nervous system responds to, and conscious of nothing else; or that because when we react upon light we are conscious of a bright color, it is this bright color that we react upon. The light reacted upon must have a direction and a motion, neither of which appears in the bright color; or are we seriously expected to believe that when a plant reacts differently on light of different rates of vibration it reacts on different colors as the human eye perceives them, and perceives the very same without eyes? Yet Mr. Holt says that animal psychology is a more solid science than human psychology because by seeing what animals react upon we can see at once what they feel, whereas tiresome people who talk might tell us they felt something different. And I think that the science of animal behavior is, indeed, more solid than descriptive ethics; because when an animal reacts on colors, it is easy to translate that stimulus and that reaction into mechanical terms, abstracting from those of our own perception; whereas in descriptive ethics our private prejudices are hard to drop, and the mechanical equivalent for a code of honor or an ascetic discipline escapes us altogether.

Mr. Holt runs into these extravagances in order to avoid

"introjection"; but I think his conception of pure or neutral being affords a simpler means of avoiding it, if we admit—what the wise have long known—that experience is full of unsubstantial objects, that is, of pure or neutral beings not embodied in the material environment to which the nervous system responds. This would not require us to say that these unsubstantial objects—dreams, fictions, secondary qualities, mathematical and formal entities— are in the mind, much less (absurd phrase) that they are made of mental stuff. The unsubstantial is made of nothing; and to speak of the stuff that dreams are made of, or of the very coinage of the brain, is to speak of what is coined or made of nothing, since like the unsubstantial fabric of a vision it leaves not a wrack behind. Consciousness itself is unsubstantial and not only is made of no stuff, but has no filling; and the phrase "contents of consciousness" is a clumsy and misleading metaphor, taken too seriously by the Germans. Mind can have no contents, but only objects. Of course, I should not *take it into my head* to quarrel with such idioms as that things *occupy the attention, come into one's mind,* or *fill one's thoughts;* but no one blessed with a little mercy towards language would press these metaphors so hard as to infer that ideas or dreams or arguments were so many gold-fish made of attention-stuff, swimming in a consciousness that filled the bowl of a skull. Words are feathery things not made to be pressed, but to be sent back and forth lightly and smartly, like a shuttlecock; and philosophers who press them in search of accuracy only pound them to death. We say loosely that things are in the mind when they are nowhere; and what leads us into that way of speaking is the fact that these homeless objects enter the history of the world only when somebody thinks of them and in virtue of that fact. But they remain essentially what they are severally—music music, mathematics mathematics, angels angels—and are not mental in substance, locus, or ontological relations; for to enter the history of this world is not ontologically necessary to any timeless and merely formal thing.

However much we may strive to identify consciousness with its objects, if we admit that consciousness exists at all, we must admit, I suppose, that it makes a new group or specious unit out of those objects. Selection individuates the part selected. What is excluded, though it remains in being just as before—materially, if its being was material, logically, if its being was logical—does not attain that sort of intensity or actuality which attention bestows on the conscious part. If the new realists deny this, would they not do better not to attempt a definition of consciousness at all, but to deny that it is definable, because like being it is universal? If what the nervous system selects is not thereby suffused with any specious unity, emphasis, or luminosity which it did not have before, must we not assume that all being, and every possible cross-section of it, vibrates with consciousness, and that every quality, proposition, and term carries with it the perpetual apprehension and assertion of itself? In that case the nervous system would do nothing for consciousness, and we ought to agree with M. Bergson that it is not an organ of consciousness at all, but only of motion. But then what a mystery it becomes, or rather what a contradiction, that consciousness should actually carve out the parts of being that the nervous system responds to, and should surround them with a false darkness!

"A navigator," Mr. Holt writes, "exploring his course at night with the help of a searchlight illuminates a considerable expanse of wave and cloud . . . and other objects that lie above the horizon. Now the sum total of all *surfaces* thus illuminated . . . is defined, of course, by the contours and surface composition of the region . . . and by the searchlight and its movement, and by the progress of the ship. The manifold so defined, however, is neither ship nor searchlight, nor any part of them, but is a portion (oddly selected) of the region through which the ship is passing. This cross-section, as a manifold, is clearly extended in space, and extended in time as well, since it extends through some watches of the night. It includes also color qualities. This cross-section, furthermore, is in no sense inside the searchlight, nor are the objects that make up the cross-section in any way dependent on the searchlight for their substance or their *being*" (p. 171). This simile expresses admirably the manner in which the field of external perception is unfolded as we live; and we need not quarrel with the fact that the name consciousness is not given, as we should have given it, to the light issuing from the lantern, but rather to the things on which it falls. That is, after all, a matter of language, though not unimportant, since it favors the silent elimination of actual consciousness from the problem. What is to be noted is that a searchlight playing on things divides them physically into a lighted and a dark portion, as the sunlight does the moon; and this de-marcation is obvious to any bystander. When the light of thought, however, or even of vision, falls on half an ob-ject, no dividing line whatever is visible to a third person between the two halves. Besides, the simile does not ex-press well the manner in which things lapse from the field of attention or are sustained in it. This field is more like the wake of the ship, or the luminous tail of a comet, with a sharp nucleus forward, where attention bites, and a vague disheveled trail behind, in which some elements are pro-longed or keep reappearing, and others go under at once, while many new eddies and figures are formed of them-selves. In other words, the field of consciousness, not to speak of consciousness itself, is a symphony of memories, suggestions, impulses, and inventions; it is a life and a discourse, rather than a cross-section of any external world, even of one conceived as compacted of all the logical terms and relations that might describe it.

About the unity of consciousness Mr. Holt says rather petulant things, such as that the idea of succession *is* a succession of ideas, although "the representative theory would never countenance anything so obviously true." He goes on to explain that when we imagine anything ex-tended our mind is extended, and when we imagine any-thing past, our mind is past, so that, I suppose, when we imagine something future or something unreal, our mind must be future or unreal, too. This result is instructive; it comes logically enough of identifying active cognition with passive images, and passive images with operating ma-terial objects—quicksands of confusion which are none the firmer because much modern philosophy is built upon them. In the cognition of succession there is a movement perceived, and if the elements that seem to take one another's place are called ideas, there is a given succession of ideas. But in that sense of the word idea the actual experience of succession is no idea; it is an act of apprehension, such as Mr. Holt prefers to ignore. Yet he would not maintain, I presume, that every succession of ideas, however discrete and disjoined, is an idea of succession; but why not, if one thing simply *is* the other? I know how irritating the unity of consciousness can be made. What have we not suffered from the ambiguities and the humbug hanging about a unity that unified now because it was the flash of attention or synthetic glance of apprehension itself; again because it was the nominal ego identical in all experiences, whoever might have them; a third time because it was a person that endured as events passed and gathered them one after the other in his capacious memory; once more because it was a grammar of cognition, peculiar, but essential to the human mind, which limited and strained human experience, passing it through the sieve of innate faculties; or finally because it was a creative fiat that generated all the universe and its history, according to a dumb inward demand? All these unifications except the first were speculative, and either merely nominal, or loose and not extant; and if we understand by consciousness the scattered experiences of a human being from the cradle to the grave, I should agree with Mr. Holt that the unity of consciousness has been much exaggerated, and that such unity as exists in a man's life is to be measured by the degree in which his thoughts and actions embody some coherent genius or character. The unity of apperception, however, can not be exaggerated because it is no matter of degree or quantity. It is a constitutive form, as forms of articulation constitute words, and what is not subject to it simply does not enter the mind. It is the mental counterpart to the response of the nervous system. To think you have composed consciousness by collecting its objects is like thinking you have created knowledge by collecting a library. Mr. Holt overlooks the mental expression of animal responses because throughout he understands by consciousness not awakened attention contrasted with unconsciousness, but the group of objects noticed contrasted with all else that lies in the field of being. Now to be gathered into a library distinguishes a group of books from all others quite as effectually as to be read, chewed, and inwardly digested. In fact it distinguishes them better: because it is easy to discover what volumes have or have not their place upon certain shelves, but who shall say what mastication, digestive juices, forgetfulness, and spontaneous variation may have let into a man's mind in reading? How much simpler, then, to maintain boldly that reading does not exist, but only book-buying, and that consciousness is not any inward difference between feeling and not feeling, noticing and not noticing anything, but is that collection of things which secure a response from the nervous system, as a library is that collection of books which have secured a nervous response from the book-buyer. Yet is it not a pity that to make things simpler, or to satisfy a mania for "monism" and a certain joy in originality, the heart-searching discoveries of German philosophy should be hushed up? For no serious attempt is made to refute or to reinterpret them; they are simply flouted.

By this unconcern we undoubtedly rid ourselves of something inconvenient in the theory of knowledge, whether the image, or the thing, or knowledge itself is not quite clear, and perhaps ought not to be asked; at any rate, we avoid dualism and the representative theory. What are these? Anyone who sees a difference between one thing and anything else is, in one sense, a dualist, and at the same time a monist, since he sees a relation between the two things. In this particular case, however, is dualism the doctrine that the act of knowing is one thing and the thing known is another? Or is it rather the doctrine that knowledge of things is impossible because they are screened from us by ideas in the mind, which, as Berkeley and Kant taught, are the *only* objects of knowledge? The latter sort of dualism should indeed be short-lived since, if ideas are the *only* objects of knowledge, things ought never to have been heard of, and may be dropped. But Mr. Holt says (justly, I think) that ideas are a special sort of thing; so that a dualism between material things and ideas, each taken as a distinct group of logical beings, is not impugned by him. Representation, too, is admitted in the sense that one object may be the sign of another, as writing is of speech; but in admitting this Mr. Holt adds that a symbol can represent nothing in the thing symbolized save what is identical in the two; as a map or a photograph represents the distribution of parts, but not the size of the

original. To be represented a thing must be reproduced
bodily, it can not be merely suggested. Nevertheless a
photograph by its chiaroscuro, and a map by conventional
tints, outlines, or numbers, represent the relief of the object without reproducing it; and a written word, which
reproduces only the order of elements in the spoken word
(and this only if we disregard diphthongs, silent letters,
and other anomalies) nevertheless suggests the sound,
which it does not reproduce. Do the individual letters
represent or do they not represent the wholly different
individual sounds which we utter when we read them?
If a sign represents only such elements in the original as
it reproduces, I hardly see how it conveys anything further
than what it is bodily, or how it remains a symbol at all
rather than a smaller and intransitive original in its own
person. Whatever use of the term representation we choose
to adopt, whence does consciousness fetch the heteroge-
neous supplementary elements which are undoubtedly
evoked? I should agree with Mr. Holt or with any critic
of psychological association that it would be silly to say,
meaning it literally, that the mind furnished these supple-
ments. *Nemo dat quod non habet;* and until the association has operated and hatched the image afresh, the mind
does not have that image to give. Doubtless it is the machinery of the brain that from time to time gives birth
to it, as the atmosphere gives birth from time to time to
"identical" flashes of lightning; but that carries us even
farther away from the given symbol.

All this, however, is but a minor complication in our
author's argument. The chief offense which representative

knowledge gives him, and gives all the immediatists, is not that it is representative, but that it is knowledge. One object, they admit, may represent another, but that an idea or thought that has none of the qualities of its object should know and describe that object is what altogether confounds them. Of course, if thought is ignored and the word idea is used passively and intransitively as Berkeley used it, for an image or a definition, an idea can not know anything different from itself, nor anything identical with itself, nor anything whatever. It is not cognitive at all, not being a consciousness or spirit, but only an object or term. Idea, however, in psychology is properly a transitive term like opinion or sensation indicating an operation of the mind upon an object, not the dead object itself; it is the act of conceiving, as sensation is the act of feeling. In this active sense neither ideas nor sensations can resemble, in any pertinent respect, that which they know or feel. They are cognitive or intellectual experiments, having intent, scope, and intensity, but no more identical with their objects than shots are identical with their targets; and I do not observe that a shot, in order to hit, has to become like its target in color, shape, or substance. Of course, if people insist that intelligence, or the faculty of knowing, can not exist, because they can give no account of it, and that, therefore, all men and angels must be without it, and are doubly fools if they pretend to have such a thing, we can only bow our heads; yet the aversion of recent philosophy from intelligence can not destroy intelligence, so long as life continues to find its expression in it. If logic and psychology unite in proving that it is impossible to be a mind, because everything must be an object or a set of objects, logic and psychology must permit the mindful few to disregard them: for a thing is possible enough if it occurs.

To cut Gordian knots in this fashion, by denying some chief element in the situation, is more dazzling than satisfactory: witness how the idealistic solution, that makes everything so easy by denying the existence of external things, has left us chafing and returning to our vomit. All the religions and philosophies in the world leave the world still standing, and soon seem a very little thing in it. Many years ago the Scotch realists decided to purge away the ideas; but since that medicine took no effect, the American realists have now decided to double the dose, and to abolish the mind as well, telling us that what we call ideas and what we call minds are simply parts or collections of objects. I suspect that what seems to some of us the blindness of this procedure seems rational courage to these realists only because, in spite of their name, they are still idealists at the back of their heads. Mr. Holt speaks (preface, p. xi) of the "concrete whole of experience," meaning, apparently, the whole universe. Yet the universe, according to his explicit doctrine, is independent of experience and far outruns it on every side, so that it can be called the world of experience only by accident, because experience has touched a corner of it, as America might be called the world of Columbus. Yet when it is instinctively named "the concrete whole of experience," I suspect that it is being identified with experience as a whole, and that we are being pulled back into absolute idealism, from which this sort of realism has not really cut loose. For if actual consciousness was assumed at the beginning as an unquestionable correlate of all being, one can see why the need of actual consciousness should not be felt when the field of view of some particular animal is considered. If the group of things perceived by that animal could be somehow delimitated, the mental presence of that group need then give us no further pause, since mental presence was assumed to be native to all being from the beginning. If this suspicion of mine is unjust, I should be glad to have it dispelled; but how else are we to explain that a whole book should be written on the concept of consciousness, and the concept of actual consciousness should not once be broached in it?

The identification of actual things with the form or description of them leads to another paradox, with which all the new realists seem especially pleased, namely, that various minds, in knowing the same thing, know one another, and are, to that extent, the same mind. If a mind is its images, and its images are its object, a mind evidently can know nothing but itself (again the most orthodox idealism) and when two minds are identical, in that they have the same object, each in knowing itself knows the other also, and no less directly, although, it must be confessed, without knowing that it does so. If when Othello and Leontes are jealous the quality of their jealousy is the same, their two consciousnesses will be, in so far, identical; and as they know the same thing they are in so far the same thing and know and are one another. This will not prevent each of them, I conceive, from remaining perfectly ignorant of the existence of the other or of the fact that the other was ever jealous; though the quality of jealousy which each has endured may be the same.

This new philosophy, then, is certainly not out of the wood, but it has cleared some hopeful paths in it. It posits a whole realm of neutral or essential being; it reasserts that truth, form, and material existence are independent of knowledge; and it places consciousness, after all, on a different level from its objects, since it admits that consciousness comes and goes, not with these objects, but with an animal reaction upon them. Mr. Holt in particular has a sense for the pathos of the natural world, in its intelligible structure and tragic fertility, a sense which makes him rise sometimes from his needless paradoxes and controversial spleen into a sincere eloquence. "I have asserted these ideas," he says (pp. 257-258), "to be mere vague nuclei of neutral entities, denizens at large of my ridiculous realm of being, non-vital, unreal, untrue, and un-everything else save un-being. . . . But the *meanings* I have intended are just those things that we meet every day—both small and large, vague and clear, faint and glaring, soft and harsh, pleasant and agonizing, living and dead." Forgetful and reckless as this philosophy may be, and partly because it is rather forgetful and reckless, I feel that it is the coming philosophy: I say *coming*, not *coming to stay*. Philosophies come and go not for their truth or falsehood, but for emphasizing and extending insights prevalent in particular circles or ages. The next age or circle finds that emphasis wanton and that extension extravagant; something else, it feels, is what is really obvious and typical. A hundred years ago people could be enthralled by the idea that the universe and all that therein is were simply terms in their personal experience, created and projected by a lurid genius struggling in their heart. We are no longer so romantic; yet, in our democratic humility, some of us are secretly sentimental; and it melts us to be told that nature, falsely thought mechanical by our heartless elders, is the work of a tender genius, not personal or lurid now, but laborious, crawling, and multitudinous, which is making, with a mother's pangs, for a life all growth and love. A vitalist, evolutionary, mystical philosophy is accordingly not without its vogue. In America, however—and this is very significant, because the new America is simply modernism unencumbered—the shrill note of mechanical action and the shrill intelligence adapted to it dominate everything else; and a philosophy which sees in outer things the obvious and typical reality and in the mind merely the same outer things in so far as they are responded to in action, is just the philosophy, I should say, to catch the ear of the times; for only those who are docile to their age are able to instruct it. Besides, these external things are conceived at once pictorially, to conciliate the impressionists, and algebraically, to conciliate the calculators. Error is identified pragmatically with failure and with buried opinions—so that if I foresaw and refuted a coming superstition, it is I that should be refuted by it and proved superstitious—and purpose is identified with presumable destiny or movement in any assignable direction; identifications which are also very modern and American in spirit. All this is, in a sense, as it should be. Other insights have had and will have their innings; and it would be unreasonable to demand spiritual concentration or great flights of thought from those whose cue is to deny thought and spirit, or to explain them away. But how deny or explain away actual thinking? Simply by identifying thought with its immediate objects, and then looking for these objects in the texture of the material world. Hence a double inquiry forces itself upon this school, an inquiry for which it is well equipped and for which the moment is propitious; namely, to analyze more sharply than any one has yet done both the immediate objects of experience and the texture of matter. Given a scrupulous inventory of each of these spheres (including the logical, non-substantive penumbra of relations surrounding them, and of things that may be truly said of them) it would be easy to confront the two and see if one is really a portion of the other. Meantime, whatever the result might be on that issue, science would have gained a closer view into some dark corners of nature.

ON IMMORTALITY

The Shade of the Stranger

What a simple thing death is, when once we are beyond it! It changes nothing but the landscape, and even that less than might be expected. All those babbling theories of ours in the upper world were curiously hasty. People who clung passionately to life, knowing rather little of it, were sure of a heaven to come; while those who were sick of life, not having lived as they should, were sure of annihilation: and it turns out that the one illusion of hope was as false as the other. If I could only show those silly optimists and cocksure naturalists these posthumous facts (though they will discover them soon enough in person) I should enjoy their discomfiture at finding themselves in a world for which they were so intentionally unprepared. Who would have credited it, that the truth about an after-life should not be some figurative rationalistic immortality, nor some foul half-witted survival of the spiritualistic sort, nor yet simple extinction, but rather this most worn and conventional of fables—old Charon and his bark? Some telepathy that our psychologists had no notion of must have guided the poets, or else the report of some traveler, like Theseus, actually returned from the dead, or perhaps there were seers and Sibyls really inspired—so many discredited traditions are turning out to be accurate after all. At any rate, here he is, a plain fact of sense, the great hoary boatman, with his portentous oar and his grisly beard, like that of Michelangelo's Moses, streaming in the blast. My fellow-passengers, too, are absolutely true to convention; huddled together timorously, like madmen alone in public, each lost in his imagined business and unconscious of the stars or pity of the world. Have I, too, I wonder, the same wild abstracted air? Inwardly, at least, I feel no tragic change. The transition from life to death, in my case, has certainly been easy and insensible. I fell asleep on my bed last night as usual, after having read in a soporific poet as much as was required for that purpose. My window was open to the stars, and my heart also: but apparently fate was not to waft me in that direction. Now the doctors are doubtless speaking of valvular failure of the heart, and my pious relations, though with some misgivings, are having masses said for my soul; but I fear the grace they are charitably calling down upon me will have to rebound undiminished upon their own heads. However, I find my condition decidedly tolerable, though I might prefer a landscape somewhat less watery, nebulous, and crepuscular. Providentially enough (perhaps everything is going to be providential now) we seem to be approaching land. What a prodigious fellow this Charon is! With what a magnificent stroke he has plunged his oar deep into the oozy bottom, and pinned the whole huge raft securely to the bank! There go my companions pell-mell ashore, like so many frightened geese. They seem to know their destination and to be in a wild haste to reach it; as for me, I have no idea where I am bound. I feel no inclination to go wading aimlessly among the trodden weeds of those dismal marshes. Am I expected to remain here alone with my gaunt ferryman? After all, the possible anger of a God is less terrible than the hopeless desolation and dumbness of this wilderness. In spite of his frowning and his incredible strength, he too seems to betray a certain uneasiness. If I tremble in his presence, perhaps he is a bit embarrassed in mine. Being a God, he ought to know my necessities before I ask, and see how opportune a revelation would now be for my guidance.

Charon (In a voice like uncertain thunder)
Oarsman I am, not guide. My bodiless freight
Is but a flight of shades, fools that on earth
Chose their wild ways, and here like snow-flakes drift
Each to his self-appointed melting-place.

The Stranger
What a voice! Evidently it is so, formidable Sir, with the others; but in my case something must have gone wrong. The Gods of the place from which I come have given me no directions. Could they possibly have intended that I should learn of you?

Charon
Can the Gods teach a mortal? How shouldst thou,

Pale puny buzz-brain, learn my art of me?
Couldst single-handed urge and steer this hulk,
Darkling, from bank to bank, through floods of lead?
Couldst, uncomplaining and unwearied, ply
One brief perpetual round?

The Stranger
What a pother I have brought about my ears for not
expressing myself properly. Is this second life too one of
misunderstanding? I had no desire whatever to learn your
art—heaven forbid! I only wished to learn my destination.

Charon
Blind, blind, blind, blind. What thine own hand has
   written
Why should I read to thee? You fluttering souls,
Like the penumbra of some circling planet
Thrown on the void, must sweep the infinite
In futile haste, as once your orbits ran.
They only know their place who choose it not.
Thou, wilting, choosing canst not rest in peace;
Thy thoughts are still atwitter, and thy crumbs
Only half munched; thy little eyes squint on.
Ask them for counsel, and hop here or there
Into what trap thou wilt.

The Stranger
If I am still alive, how is it that I am here? Or am I
not here, but only dreaming?

Charon

Thought travels with its object. Thou art here
If thy heart's here; yet thou mayst turn away
To flare a moment in some spurt of life
'Mid the quick shifts of the world. Thou art not free
From mind's forced freedom: canst not choose but
choose.

The Stranger

In spite of the liberty you attribute to me, I cannot
shake off this illusion, if it be one. Perhaps if I act it out
it will vanish of itself, like the illusions of love. The place
seems not uninviting. I see walls and paths upon those
hillsides, among oaks and cypresses and olives. This might
be the point of Stamboul at sunset, or the Aventine or
the Caelius, in their former pleasant desolation. O penetrating charm of golden light and quietness, and silent
people, beggars, antiquaries, belated saints, people with
souls; and walled, neglected gardens, and noble, spacious,
still-inhabited ruins!

Charon

The hound is on the blood-scent. What they loved
Fastens fond mortals to the ghost of the earth
Whence what they loved is fled.—Leap, fool, ashore.
This is thine Island of Remembrance. Here
All seem to walk whom thou art mindful of.

The Stranger (leaping from the bark)

What happiness! I have reached my destination.

Charon

Poor babbler. Harken to an oracle
And ponder it well. To the eternal shore
They who sail know it not, and they who explore
Come not in truth, until they sail once more.

The Stranger

Then you yourself, hoary deity, who are thundering
these solemn things, are not really here and I am not really
dead? You laugh? Or is it I that am laughing at myself?
I will leave this mystery to be solved for me at my second
coming, when I shall not know I am here. This time, not
being here in truth, I may enjoy the incomparable spectacle. The place is firm underfoot and green overhead.
Let me explore.